A New Kind of Normal

Unlocking the Medium within

Kerrie Wearing

What people are saying about *A New Kind of Normal.*

"Kerrie isn't just an extraordinary Medium, she's one of the few I have met who comes from the heart, not now and again but ALL the time and is passionate about sharing her experiences. She never switches off and is always ready to help those around her, which is exactly what this book is about, helping those around her. I'm often asked 'how do I move forward' Kerrie's book will be among my recommendations for all who ask that question."

~David Wells~
Medium, Astrologer, Past Life Therapist and Qabalist

"Kerrie Wearing has written the most awe-inspiring guide to connecting to your God-given intuitive talent and abilities. Follow her guidance and you'll always have the perfect answers at the perfect time delivered in the most perfect way."

~Peggy McColl~
New York Times Best-Selling Author

"A New Kind of Normal is a wondrous blend of sincerity, wisdom and practicality. Kerrie Wearing offers her spiritual insights in an incredibly matter-of-fact manner; she takes what has been historically considered as intangible and mystical, and brings it firmly into the realms of accessible and normal. A great read for the intelligent spiritual explorer."

~Kim Forrester~
Spiritual Commentator

Copyright © 2012 by Kerrie Wearing
All rights reserved. This book or any portion thereof may not be reproduced or used in any manner whatsoever without the express written permission of the publisher except for the use of brief quotations in a book review.

Printed in Australia

First Printing 2012

ISBN 978-0-9874527-0-2

inSpirit Publishing
28 Hickson Circuit
Harrington Park NSW 2567
Australia
www.inSpiritpublishing.net

This book is dedicated to

Allen Murray

My brother, your short life has provided so much.

I owe you Bro.

A New Kind of Normal

Unlocking the Medium within

Kerrie Wearing

I offer you peace.

I offer you love.

I offer you friendship.

I see your beauty.

I hear your need.

I feel your feelings.

My wisdom flows from the Highest Source.

I salute that Source in you.

Let us work together for unity and love.

~Mahatma Gandhi.

Contents

Introduction	8
What is Normal Anyway?	12
Preparing the Channel	24
It's all about Energy	32
~Composition of the Human Energy field	35
~Seeing and Feeling the Aura	37
~Energetic Protection and Grounding	63
Reaching your Highest Potential	69
Their World is our World	82
Understanding your Spiritual Abilities	89
Living with Spirit	111
~Interpreting the Message	120
Your Spirit Team	127
Developing your New Talent	139
Haunted Access	153
The Psychic Child	161
Servitude is more than an Attitude	167
Acknowledgements	173
About the Author	176

Introduction

Is it really possible for each and everyone of us to be psychic and embrace a life of living with Spirit, and to communicate with the afterlife in a way that identifies us as a psychic medium. I certainly believe so and hope that after reading this book you will too.

You see, I was not born with any more natural psychic talent than the next person. I didn't see dead people as a child nor did I make psychic predictions. My story begins much like yours, a little girl growing up in Sydney Australia, the oldest child in a single parent family. It wasn't until the age of twenty six, through a series of tragic events did I discover there was more to life as I knew, and that we could learn to be psychic.

This concept captured my attention and very quickly became a passion, as I found that developing my psychic abilities and awakening my spirituality gave me a sense of purpose I didn't have before. Life became more exciting, inspiring and filled with the unexpected as I slowly discovered who I was, began unfolding a whole new me and

Introduction

embraced a new kind of normal. Life still presented challenges, however I found in those challenges that I began to really learn about myself and my place in this world, giving me a clear sense of direction and filling a void in my heart.

Using our psychic senses is an inherent part of who we are as humans and with the afterlife around us at all times, it only takes an intention and willingness on our part to open ourselves to this beautiful, loving world of energy. If you are willing to put in the time and effort, then this book, its tools and techniques will most definitely assist you to develop your ability to communicate with Spirit and unfold your own Spirit.

Did you know that the biggest challenge people face when learning to meditate is how to overcome their mind chatter? This was my initial challenge too and I share with you my secret in stemming the incessant flow of thought. I help you to discover the secrets to unlocking your clairvoyance, clairaudience and clairsentience as the techniques provided will highlight your strengths and keep it simple for you. Did you also know that the feeling sense of clairsentience is the most common ability of all, especially in children? Learn how this natural ability can sometimes have adverse effects on your own energy levels and how to gain control over this, so that next time you are in a shopping centre or large crowd, you no longer feel drained of all your energy.

It is time to reach forward into a new awareness and find your story. Find your purpose and the meaning of life for you. I share my story and my knowledge of Mediumship in the hope that you may benefit from my experience and the pages in between. Now is not the time to be standing in the wings, but to step out onto the stage that is your life. As I mentioned before, life will continue to present us with its challenges but through our growth we can find new ways of dealing with them. You see, the real purpose of working with Spirit is the very personal journey of spiritual evolution. The guidance we receive will always lead us forward into experience which can provide us with insight and understanding regarding our own soul, our own spirit, and who we are. This, you will find is an enigmatic discovery as you begin working with your Spirit Guides. It is their unspoken purpose in working with you.

Hear what others are really saying to you with their energy as your newfound awareness is applied in your day to day living. Increase your understanding of who to trust and who not to, feel the pain of others and employ more empathy as you find a new level of sensitivity opening up. My children are often perplexed as to why I'm crying over something on TV or why my mood might fluctuate quite drastically. These are often the repercussions of being psychically sensitive to energy, which will also unfold for you as I share with you the nature of the human energy field and help you to increase your awareness of this. How can we perceive the energy of the afterlife, if at first we do not understand where our own energy begins and ends.

With my work as a psychic medium, I feel that my true purpose with this work is as a teacher, using mediumship as a tool to assist people to unfold their spiritual and personal growth. In an effort to truly assist you with this objective in mind, there are many exercises and suggestions in how to apply your new knowledge throughout the book. Often it takes a while to find your "thing", but know that in trying a few different avenues and learning what is not for you, you are stepping closer to finding what is.

It's also important that we discuss some of the more popular topics within the arena of mediumship, such as protection, hauntings and psychic children. While my beliefs can often been seen as controversial, I say to you that these are my beliefs as I've come to learn and experience them throughout my individual development. I share them with you in the hope that they may answer some questions for you. I do specify however, that it is ok if these beliefs differ from what

Introduction

your thoughts are right now.

Ethics is another important topic not to be overlooked. While I am sharing with you many of the secrets of mediumship and do genuinely wish for you a life living with Spirit, I do not believe that every person is meant to be a professional medium. It is important to acknowledge that many of you may try and I want you to know that it is all too common an occurance for a psychic to put themselves out in the professional arena too soon and before they most likely should. Ethics, integrity and our sense of servitude are all values and understandings that need to be at the forefront of any psychic's work. The responsibility of offering information, insight to another, and the responsibility of speaking on behalf of another soul, is a huge undertaking and deserving of the greatest level of respect.

Throughout this book, some of what we discuss may resonate with you as you find yourself thinking *"Yeah, I think I knew that"* or *"You know, that really feels right"*. Other times you may completely disagree. And that's ok. Everything I share with you in this book, all the understandings and learnings are my own personal truth. Developed through my own journey with the guidance of Spirit, all this I have shared and used to teach others for many years now, assisting many of those who have come to understand their own purpose and some who now work professionally within the Australian psychic industry.

In my experience, all there is, is our own truth. So please use this book to inspire your own truth. If something does not sit right, question it and find it within yourself to understand why. Going within in such a way, will have you living with Spirit and eloquently unfolding your very own new kind of normal.

What is Normal Anyway?

> Live a life less ordinary
> Live a life extraordinary with me
> Live a life less sedentary
> Live a life evolutionary with me
> ~**Carbonleaf.**

As a little girl one of my favourite television programs was Eight is Enough, at the height of its success the family loses their mother through illness and battle with their grief, in time welcoming a new step mother. Through out of all this the coming together of this family unit warmed my heart as the Bradfords stirred the imaginings of a little girl. My own upbringing was in stark contrast to the warm, heartfelt yet sometimes funny relationships played out by the eight siblings. Growing up in the suburbs of Sydney, Australia, my reality was quite different from the TV family I longed for.

My parents having divorced when I was three years of age and as the oldest of two children, I found early on that responsibility was a way of life for me, while aware that my brother and I required food, shelter and the basic necessities, my mother's ability to express love and nurturing was somewhat inhibited. During my formative years, it was a usual part of our weekly routine to find her leave us for the comfort of the local drinking establishment. We found ourselves reliant on a babysitter, until in her eyes I was old enough to take on this responsibility.

What is Normal Anyway?

At 11 years of age, it became my job to take care of both of us on these nights while my mother, a single parent continued to enjoy her social life. My young mind often struggled to comprehend the need for this, especially in times when money was tight and we were going without. Then there were the times when a young girl just wants her mother's love and attention. Many times we argued as I got older, and for my cries of *"We need you here more than the Club does"* to fall on deaf ears.

My brother Allen, was not an easy child to look after. He was a handful for mum and other adult relatives, let alone for me too. The time he started a fire at the end of Mum's bed is a part of family storytelling, as is the time, he once put himself in the shower and locked the door while mum was out one afternoon. After a while, I started to think that he had been in there a long time, only to find that when I finally checked on him, he had climbed out the window to go and play with his friends. This kind of responsibility coupled with the need to self-parent when it came to my schooling, early in life created a large part of who I was. It left me with many characteristics I would later change, as my spirituality awakened my awareness to who I was as a person.

During this early time my emotional challenges were many. I often retreated into myself from not having my needs met, or from being verbally attacked should I be brave enough to express myself. There were many times when we received verbal and physical attacks as Mum's way to discipline was to hit first and ask questions later. I used to start crying even before I was hit, though my brother would sometimes laugh which was never a good move. Sadly though, I adopted some of this form of discipline and would often try to manage my brother the same way. While as a child I didn't know any better, it still hurts me now to know that in some ways Allen really had two mothers, not a mother and a sister.

School was not easy for me either, my struggles to relate to my family at home often transpired to my schooling as I struggled to make friends. It would take me a long time to overcome my shyness and build trust in the friends I did make, only to find that we would be moving house and therefore schools as well. This was a theme throughout my childhood with most of these moves prompted by financial difficulties for my mother. This trait of taking a long time to make friends and build trust is something that still exists for me today. Only, I now find it serves me well and true friends understand this about me.

Throughout these formative years I learnt to rely strongly upon myself, growing an inner strength that is still such a steadfast part of who I am, that it is difficult to fathom myself without it. I saw through the weakness of others and inherently knew that in being who I am, comes a strength that often others find difficult to work with. While I never perceived this until my later years, it has always been there, from the darker more challenging beginnings to the wondrous life I lead now. You see, it's the one thing that has served me always, and while that often made life difficult, it is not something I have ever shied away from. Being me is all I can be, even if that me has changed and transformed monumentally over the years.

I hear you asking *"Ok, this is all some great insight into who I am as a person and my childhood, but what about my psychic experiences?"* How did they factor into all this? Well, I'd love to be able to tell you that as a child I saw dead people and made some pretty spectacular psychic predictions. But I can't. You see, in this area as a child I was no different than the next person. No different to you right now perhaps. It wasn't until I was twenty six that my spirituality and love of all things psychic would come to the fore.

From these early years I can recall that around the age of ten or eleven regularly seeing a white horse and a man in a trench coat while I was trying to go to sleep. Looking back, this didn't last long and is hard to tell whether this was Spirit or imagination. Though with my understanding of Spirit now, I would suggest that these projections were based in fear and not Spirit. Firstly, these images didn't say or do anything, they were just there in my room and secondly, I trust that with my senses now I would feel a spirit connection to it as I write this. The feeling is one of emptiness, so I'm sure that they were mental projections from a scared little girl. We moved again not long after this, which settled things for me as I enjoyed playing Monopoly quite often with our new border. A little quality attention can do wonders.

If there is one person in my childhood who influenced me spiritually at all, it would be my grandmother. I often stayed with my mum's mum during school holidays, and each Sunday morning we would both walk down to the end of her street, crossing the road to attend the morning mass service at the local Catholic Church. There are really two things which have stayed with me about this time from my Nan. One, was her level of commitment. Every Sunday, without failure she would rise at 6am, taking her time to have breakfast, dress and enjoy the walk to Church. This commitment to her faith was still evident as she became ill and could no longer attend church, where she would have the priest visit her every week for a blessing, telling me that if you did this every week before you died then Mother Mary would visit you on your deathbed. I sincerely hope that this did happen for her and I should make a mental note to ask her next time she pops in for chat. Secondly, I can still quite vividly remember her telling me one Sunday, as we entered the grounds of the church that eventually everyone comes back to God. I'm sure she was telling me as I was starting to make some noise about not wanting to attend church any more. In my case she was right, the spiritual guidance Nan gave continues today with her being a loving member of my Spirit team, often relaying loving guidance and understanding about my own life, although I still miss our chats over a cup of tea and a piece fruit flan, her favourite.

Moving into high school was even more challenging. My struggle with finding friends continued and so too, did the moving house and schools. It wasn't until my senior years that I finally made some lasting friendships which still exist today. Puberty and adolescence was a very unsettling time, as it is for most teenagers. However with my lack of good role models and an inept emotional security, my desires for a loving family got easily directed towards boys and it wasn't long before I was giving of myself in the hope of being loved in return. My first serious boyfriend, while good looking lacked his own emotional security that manifested in jealousy. I wasn't allowed to even have a poster on my wall of George Michael without him getting angry with me. It was the eighties remember, and Wham were a favourite. This relationship ended not long after we got engaged. Young, at seventeen and thinking that the engagement would prove to him how much I loved him and he needn't feel insecure. Well, I'm sure you can easily guess how well that worked. I am however, forever grateful for the insights I learned regarding jealousies and insecurities from that relationship. It certainly helped me going forward with new relationships to be clear on what would work for me in those areas.

It wasn't too long after this that I encountered what I recognise as my first psychic experience. This came in the form of a dream, highlighting to me a premonition that soon became reality. In the dream, I was standing outside a night club talking with a friend when the boy I was dating drove up and got out of a car with another girl, who was being quite friendly. He had been at a party and we were to meet at the nightclub later. This event played itself out exactly as I had dreamt it, and suffice to say that relationship was no longer. This dream stands out as the one and only psychic experience known to me, prior to March 1996.

Around this time I explored the Pentecostal Christian movement a little. My belief in God was something that has always been a part of who I am. It was never a question as to whether God exists or not, only finding the right interpretation of that relationship for me. Having early on found that the Catholic faith didn't connect with my soul, it didn't take me long to discover that neither did the born again Christian faith. I found their preaching too frightening, leaving me with little or no hope for the future as they often talked about the end of the world coming, and only the Christians being saved by God to live in heaven. For a young eighteen year old this was too much to deal with, and whether these teachings are symbolic or literal was never explained, nor was how you really "hear" God. These understandings would not come until much later.

Throughout this book when I refer to the term God, please know that it could just as easily be called the Universe, Great Spirit, the Divine or whichever term you feel most comfortable using. For me, God is within each one of us and when we all operate from that part of us which is connected to the Divine, then we have an omnipresent source of creation most us of refer to as God.

The following years saw me grow into young adulthood and achieve many of the things most young people do. A prosperous career in banking and administration with some great friends and an active social life. My independence was surging forth and as a result I was becoming more settled in who I was. Life was great! There was really only one thing that wasn't working so well. My low self esteem and how that manifested itself when it came to men. I was still giving of myself too much in the hope of being loved, only to find that my heart was breaking each time I was let down. At one point, I made a conscious decision to respect myself more, slow down and approach my love life more in control.

It wasn't long after this that I started to see a friend I worked with in the bank quite differently. I started to notice his sense of humour more along with his willingness to help others as our love-hate relationship started to blossom into something decidedly more friendly. Then, faced with the prospect of not seeing one another again as I tendered my resignation from the bank to go and work in the city, Rod and I began dating. We were married a year later when I was 21 and quickly set about buying a home and establishing ourselves. We travelled a little, worked on our careers and just enjoyed being together. It was five years later that our first child Nathan was born.

This was the beginning of what was to be my annus horribilis, as the Queen would say. While I was pregnant with Nathan it was discovered through the routine ultrasound that his left kidney was much larger than it should have been. With the series of tests that followed, we were advised that our baby would require an operation very early on in his little life. This was not something we were prepared for, nor would you be really. It certainly changes your perspective of many things, as you realise that your little one is going to have to contend with health issues neither one of us had ever faced. This was to have a major impact on my relationships with my mum and my brother.

By this time both of them enjoyed drinking a little too much, with my brother's life now being severely affected. Allen had not been able to obtain any long term employment since leaving school and had encountered some hiccups with the law for break and entering. He also had a tendency to suicidal thoughts, as his life would spiral out of control and he would find himself in depression. Up until this point, I was still being the parent to both of them and often found myself supporting and giving endlessly to two people who wouldn't, or couldn't necessarily help themselves. Having tried to engage them both in drug and alcohol counselling, I often found my efforts to support wasted and unappreciated.

Now my needs and that of my families were changing. So I made another conscious decision to pull back some of my support and focus on my new priority - my little boy who was going to have a tough entry into this world. While Nathan's operation went as well as could be expected, for us as new parents it was extremely confronting. Firstly, with a series of tests and then with the operation itself. Nathan was operated on at eight weeks of age and had his left kidney removed which was found to have formed with cysts all over it, known as a polycystic kidney. Our reserves of emotional strength were pulled on during that time in the spring of 1994, as we dealt with what life had dealt us in the best way we could. However, little was I to know that things had only just begun and I would be needing more of those reserves quite soon.

Easter 1995 would prove to be the most heart wrenching time of my life, and yet a major turning point which over time would yield many positives. The weekend started quite well as we celebrated Nathan's first Easter even though both Rod and I were suffering with cold and flu. About midnight on the Monday night, I received a call from my brother, he was drunk and just wanted to say hi. I was a little annoyed at this, being that it was late at night and I was due to go to work the next day. We said our *"Happy Easters"*, our goodbyes and hung up. A little while later he called again, only this time I didn't answer the phone, being more frustrated with his timing. Though with hindsight I am so glad I didn't answer that call for fear of reprimanding him, because as it turned out, this was the last time I would hear my brother's voice. Later that morning we received a phone call from Mum. She was away working and had called the house to check on Allen, only to have the police answer the phone. The police wouldn't tell her what was happening so she called us and asked that Rod call the house. We had stayed home too sick to work, so Rod called and was told that Allen had taken his own life by hanging himself on the back verandah. He was twenty three at the time on the Monday and would have turned twenty four a few days later on the Friday. Instead of celebrating his birthday, we were viewing his body.

Amongst all the drama and my own grief, my need to understand his pain was never too far away. Having a childhood as we did was not easy, though I was blessed with an intelligence Allen didn't possess and a maturity far beyond my years. Yet the effects of such losses as our annual Easter holiday were deeply felt by both of us. We hadn't really enjoyed Easter as a family together since I was twelve. At that time, Mum had begun working at the Sydney Royal Easter Show which would take her away for weeks at a time before and all through Easter. When we were younger and too young to spend that kind of time on our own Mum would find friends to house us or look after us as best as she could. For us, it was not only uncomfortable but painful, as we lost a treasured childhood holiday and family time together. So for me, when my brother chose this time of year to end his life, it spoke volumes of his pain and suffering, as only two siblings can understand a similar pain.

Suicide is a unique kind of grief in its own way, that more often than not has a lot of questions attached to it. All you really want is the answer to one question. Why? For Mum, that was and still is certainly the case, but for me I always knew it lay in the childhood we both experienced. For Allen, it grew through the problems with his education, long term unemployment and extremely low self esteem. Couple this with extensive use of alcohol, marijuana and then the event that breaks the camel's back, a relationship break down. I also learnt recently, that he was the third generation of males on my father's side to have alcoholism and suicidal tendencies, therefore there must be some truth in the genetics also having an influence. Knowing and understanding all of this didn't make it any easier though, as I struggled with my own grief and being the strong one for Mum.

As is so often the situation with the universe, it seems to deal you blow after blow all in a short space of time. We were only just getting back to some sense of normalcy with this shock, when we were struck again with the unexpected passing of someone else so near and dear. My Aunt Pat was a very special person in my life right from the day I was born. At three, I had the honour of being the flower girl in her wedding which became not just a treasured memory, but somewhat of a tradition as I married and so too, her eldest daughter Cindy. When I married Rod, Aunty Pat's youngest daughter Renee was my flower girl and then when Cindy married, both of my children were involved, Jessica as flower girl and Nathan as page boy. And just to add even more special memories, the dress Renee wore at my wedding was adjusted and used by Jessica for Cindy's wedding. This connection outlines how close I was to my aunt and still am to her family. I certainly felt like a third daughter and have many memories of little visits with my aunt and uncle prior to them having children. Whether they realise or not, my aunt and uncle represented for me what I thought the ideal loving "normal" family unit should be. Many times during school holiday visits to their home did I gain an understanding of how a family can come together. The get togethers my aunt and uncle shared with their friends playing cards around the table, enjoying good times while all the kids were running around having fun in their pyjamas are not only treasured memories, but had a huge influence on a little girl who learned that this was what I wanted to. If I couldn't get it in my childhood, then that was what I would grow up to have.

Aunty Pat was only forty five when she had a fatal heart attack on Melbourne Cup Day of 1995. By now they were living in a small NSW country town which they loved, finally having seemed to find their place in life. Pat always enjoyed a good time and was excited with her plans to celebrate Australia's greatest horse race, the Melbourne Cup. It wasn't to be though, while showering her heart gave out as she left behind her husband Doug and two young beautiful girls. This event was so unexpected and happened at such a critical time for my cousins, Renee was twelve while Cindy had just turned twenty. To lose their mother at such young ages, it altered their course in life without question and it is something they still struggle with today.

For me it compounded the grief I already had. I have learnt since that grief is like a well of emotion, each time a new bucket of loss is added to that well, it stirs it all up and overflows a little, even if you are adept at emotional self healing.

There is one part of this event that now always brings a smile to my face though. It was my uncle that called me that day as I was in the middle of changing Nathan's nappy. I didn't have a cordless phone at the time, I don't think they were that popular yet. Anyway, I took the baby with me to answer the phone in the kitchen – nappyless. At some point while talking with Uncle Doug amidst all of our tears I looked down on the floor and found that the baby had relieved himself all over the carpet. Baby poop everywhere! Sometimes there really is nothing like your children to keep you grounded.

Grief, really is something that rocks your whole foundation. Losing my only brother and my aunt, who was very much a mother figure for me so close together with both of them so young, left me with a lot of questions.

I started to question the more purposeful meaning of life. I was thinking more and more about what the afterlife was. What or who was God really? I wanted peace and understanding for myself. Surprisingly, this was also coupled with a yearning to help and give back to others in some way. This was a very strong emotion at the time, though I had no idea how to go about this. All I knew was that I wanted to help those who were going through what I was, especially where suicide was concerned. Through my own efforts to find some suicide specific grief counselling, I found that there was a huge lack of resources. In 1995 throughout the whole of Sydney there was only one Survivors of Suicide group and that was on the other side of the city. Left to try some general grief counselling I found it to be fairly ineffective and not meeting my needs at all. Fifteen years later though and it is nice to report that this is all very different now. Lifeline and Suicide Prevention Australia now do excellent work in this area.

A few months later, I was discussing all of this with my oldest and dearest friend, Diane. Having known Di since I was eleven when I went to work with her in the local doctor's surgery to carry out the archiving of their filing, we have a friendship that has spanned most of my life and while we don't always see each other often, she is someone I love and treasure in my life. Diane suggested I read a book called *The Celestine Prophecy* written by *James Redfield*. This book not only provided many answers, it literally changed my life overnight. For those of you that do not know the book, it's a fictional story weaved with spiritual undertones. It taught me about the concepts of energy and how the whole universe is made of up this energy and that as humans we engage in energetic interactions all the time. It opened my eyes to the idea of synchronicity and that there is no such thing as coincidence. All this set me on a more conscious spiritual journey from that moment in March 1996. Through this book and its concepts of spirituality, I had found the meaning of life for me. My search for answers had begun in earnest and like a lot of people, I read as many books as I could get my hands on, sat in spiritual development circles and found myself attending the local spiritualist church. It was here that I would make some lasting friendships and begin to learn so much about myself as I slowly uncovered my spiritual abilities and brought about a new kind of normal.

In this chapter:
- We all live our own unique paths to spiritual awareness and living.
- Our life experiences shape our thoughts, beliefs and patterns.
- Some have a major life event such as a death of a loved one that leads you to seeking more understanding of the afterlife and spiritual understanding. For others, it is an interest, a curiosity, a stirring or a calling that gently unfolds.
- Grief is an ongoing emotion, each time a new bucket of loss is added to that well, and it stirs it all and overflows a little.
- *The Celestine Prophecy* by *James Redfield* changed my life overnight.

Preparing the Channel

> *The intuitive mind is a sacred gift*
> *and the rational mind is a faithful servant,*
> *We have created a society that honours the servant*
> *and has forgotten the gift.*
> **~Albert Einstein.**

While mediumship is perceived to be primarily about helping others with the ability a medium possesses to communicate with Spirit, by offering information that is evidential by nature, and therefore providing proof that your loved one's soul continues to exist. It really begins much deeper than that, as it centers around the understanding of one's own true nature and the all important aspect of understanding the divine connection which lies within the heart of each of us, as it is through this connection that we make the links to the afterlife and beyond. Therefore, in preparation we must first begin to become aware and understand our own personal energies. How can we know where the afterlife begins, if at first we do not know where our own individual energies begin and end. Becoming aware and maintaining your own energy is an everyday ongoing process and is best developed by giving this focus a priority in your life. There are many everyday ways to ensure you are kept in tiptop energetic and emotional shape. Most of which are just good common sense, though in working with them consciously will lead you to being a well balanced spiritual individual.

Start by asking simple questions of yourself each day. *"How do I feel today?" "Did you wake up tired and emotional?" "With a headache?" "Feeling overwhelmed?" "Is your own life suffering in any way at the moment?"* These types of factors affect all of us from time to time and need to be considered as to whether the effects are adversely impacting your energy. Being honest with yourself, and by honouring yourself in this way is the first step to greater awareness and being empowered to change what you desire to change.

To begin with meditation is a real key in developing this kind of awareness. Through meditation you will be able to become aware of your inner being and your own auric field. You will be able to become aware of the energies within your environment, the energies of Spirit and slowly become more in tune with the energies of others. It will help you to release your everyday mind and create a space to receive these understandings from within. All that is needed is for you to make a commitment to spend the time in meditation.

When I first began my psychic development study by sitting in a home circle, the first challenge I needed to overcome was learning to meditate and control the mind chatter many of us encounter. Like many of you, I have a very analytical mind prone to conceptualising and trying to understand everything before I have even fully experienced what is before me. Did you know that the mind chatter hindrance is the most common challenge initially presented when you first begin to learn to meditate? In every beginner class, you can guarantee that there are a handful of people with this question and wanting help to control it. Firstly, know that it does take a little time. It is not until the third or fourth class that as a teacher, I actually expect people to start to settle into the energies to enjoy a relaxed productive experience during meditation. Give yourself time to settle into this new experience. Try not to give up before your little miracle happens, it is a new discipline and one that improves with practice.

I was able to overcome this difficulty with some help from a friend. During that first home circle I'd made a new friend whose name is Monique. We were both new to Spirit and had new one year old baby boys in common as well. Early on we were having coffee at Monique's house when she said that she had received a message for me. If I recall correctly she was asking how to help me with meditating. In response she was told to *"give her the key."* As we were having coffee, and not long after she told me about this message, we were thumbing through a new age magazine when we had one of our first *"OMG"* moments. In the magazine was an article titled *"The Key to Meditation"*. Once we overcame our excitement at the way Spirits hand was manifesting for us and actually read the article it was extremely helpful. While I cannot recall who the author was, I would like to honour their wisdom and insight and how it has helped not just me, but many of the people I have shared the technique with as I now share it with you.

The technique is quite simple and surprisingly effective. In the early stages of your meditation begin to talk to your mind as if it were another person and lovingly ask it to be quiet. For example: *"Dear mind, I ask you to be quiet for now. I am trying to meditate and I would really appreciate your co-operation with this. I would really love you to be quiet so that I may receive some peace, harmony and understanding. I will allow you to return to your ramblings when I am finished but for now I would really love you to be quiet. Thank you".* Be sure to use your own words to that effect, however it is the love and respect you apply that yields the results. For me, this technique made all the difference from the first time I tried it, and I know the same can be said for many others.

Meditation can be achieved in a whole gamut of ways. Yes, sitting down and listening to a guided meditation is recommended from time to time, especially at the beginning of your development. However, be mindful that short stays of mindfulness are all ways to stem the flow of misguided thoughts, creating peace and harmony in a way akin to the calm before a storm. Managing your day with intervals of mindfulness and awareness of your thoughts will increase your heightened sensitivities without a doubt. Personally, I find ironing conducive to this type of mindfulness meditation for me. While I'm ironing one of Rod's business shirts or the kids jeans its never too long before I'm zoning out and finding inspiration and solutions to some of what has been crowding my thoughts with worry. The internationally recognised clairvoyant medium Lisa Williams, shared with me during her 2009 Australian tour that she meditates while showering each morning. She spends some time focusing on each of her chakras and becoming aware of how they feel each day. This is good energy housekeeping, as it then empowers Lisa to not only be aware, but to take action and change or heal whatever may come up for her during that short but powerful meditation.

The process of communicating energetically is also greatly enhanced when one works at keeping their energy physically light. This aids in the process of raising your energetic vibration and helps with the blending of your energy with that of spirit to be as seamless as possible. It is in this coming together of energy that communication takes place. This will be covered in more detail in the next chapter.

Tips to help keep your energy light
1. Keep all meals light especially in the hours leading up to communicating with Spirit.
2. Avoid alcohol, minimise caffeine and nicotine in the 24 hour period prior to when your communication is to take place. These all affect how much oxygen and energy can flow through your body.

3.   Drink lots of water. This enhances the flow of oxygen and energy through the body. Energetic work is very dehydrating, so it's important to keep yourself hydrated, so I suggest keeping a bottle of water with you when you engage in any form of working with energy.

It is important to remember that the universal energy which you use to connect to Spirit with, is filtered through you. There is no way around this, all interactions will be expressed through you and your framework of experience and knowledge. This includes filtering through your energy and those parts of you connected or disconnected to the Divine source of Love. Therefore it's imperative to work towards healing on all levels of your mind, body and soul while taking care of yourself so as to provide greater healing to those you will serve. You are but a tool of light for what needs to take place, allow it to be so to your utmost potential. With experience it is possible to put such disturbing energies aside and connect anyway, but are you going to reach the highest potential for yourself, Spirit or for the person that you may be connecting with Spirit for on their behalf.

This then highlights the need for self-healing and its role in mediumship. There is a saying that *"the best healers are those that heal themselves"*. I am a big advocate of this, and have found personally that each time I achieve a new level of understanding, or have moved through an emotional blockage of sorts, that this has directly impacted my mediumship abilities. I find that as I heal emotional burdens or negativity, this is naturally replaced with more loving Divine energy which allows my connection to Spirit to be enhanced. After such tuning, my radio station is able to pick up in stereo so to speak. The channel between myself and Spirit is much clearer resulting in a direct quantifiable improvement not only in the connection, but also in the information I am able to glean from Spirit.

In the early days of waking up spiritually, like everyone I couldn't

Preparing the Channel

seem to get enough information. I was like a sponge soaking it all in, reading books, attending development groups and joining my local spiritualist church. My thirst for information was difficult to satisfy, as too was trying to find the right teacher. The professionalism I came across was disappointing and a little surprising. That first group where I met Monique was supposed to be a twenty week course which was stopped at week eight with no real explanation. Then there was the group we would all pay weekly for, just to listen to the teachers own problems, or the two year course I signed up for with the teacher who was consistently telling us our chakras or energy centers were all functioning well. None of this sat well with me so it was never too long before I moved on. For someone who was new to what the 'new age' spiritual movement had to offer, I knew I wanted help to heal and grow but just didn't know how to go about it, and sadly the 'professionals' in the area, I found didn't really know either. The last group did however help me to achieve one thing, and that was a connection to my first spirit guide; Ralph, an English monk. Everything does happen for a reason.

By this time Monique and I had started to conduct a home circle ourselves. I look back now and think *"OMG, I really had no place doing that yet, what was I thinking?"* However it was a positive experience for all involved and we all gained a lot. It was during one of these class meditations that Ralph came to me and said *"Come with me."* Yes, by now I had developed clairvoyance and clairaudience though still didn't fully understand either. In response to Ralph I asked *"Where to?"* His reply was *"To hell and back"*. Well, that was enough to scare the hell out of me. So I said *"Ok, but not right now everyone is meditating and I need to ensure they're ok."* He must have thought what an idiot, though I'm sure he understood my fear.

This was my precursor to the first stage of my self-healing journey. Soon I began to receive messages that my mother was going to die. Of course, this scared me even more. It wasn't until much later and with some hindsight that I came to realise these messages were indicating that our relationship was going through a death and rebirth transformation primarily because of the healing work I was doing in this area. I had begun to look beyond the surface and see more of who my mother was and what had brought her to this point. Understanding her childhood pain and lack of communication ability really helped me to see things differently and release a lot of ill will towards her. In doing so, I was able to reclaim my own power and responsibility and therefore make different choices about how I relate or deal with situations that arise ongoingly with that relationship.

This was the first step in a long healing journey that was to last many, many years. Through all of it, my ability to own my contribution to this relationship as well as others has been the key to my sense of peace. Through seeing how I behaved or what I could have done differently, if anything, I have been able to walk strong in who I am with an ever growing sense of peace.

This sense of personal responsibility could be your key too. If we allow it to be, the natural process of healing one's hurts and attending to those areas of your life which detract from your peace and balance, is probably the most import thing you can do to aid in raising your vibration, helping to bring a more loving energy to any energetic healing process.

Living from your heart, honouring your Spirit and embracing all Spirit, will unfold this process naturally in your life as Spirit seeks to empower you in your life and open your heart to ever increasing amounts of love. This is the way of the Divine. As humans we only need to see it as our responsibility to take heed of this process and continually self evaluate where we are in our lives, and who we are as people evolving to.

Your first step in honouring your self healing
1. Obtain a journal and at the end of each day take some to time to write how you feel about the day. Be honest and acknowledge both the negative and the positive.
2. Try not to judge or reprimand yourself, just give voice to how you feel.
3. Now write down three things you are grateful for right now.

The aim here is for you to feel lighter simply by acknowledging your feelings. In time, you will find a greater awareness of yourself starting to take shape and a sense of empowerment as you start to recognise areas of your life you would like to see improved.

In this chapter:
- To ease mind chatter, converse with your mind and ask for it to be quiet.
- Use everyday activities such as ironing or when having a shower to practice mindfulness.
- Follow 'Tips' to keep your energy light to enhance the energetic and physical preparation needed to connect with Spirit.
- Take your first steps in honouring your self healing by starting a journal with how you feel each day, giving voice to how you feel and completing each entry with three things in your life you feel grateful for right now.

It's all about Energy

> *Compassion automatically invites you*
> *to relate with people,*
> *Because you no longer regard people*
> *as a drain on your energy.*
> **~Chogyam Trungpa.**

I soon met my first real teacher, Trish, and found that my spiritual development centered around further developing my clairvoyance and the first efforts at communicating with Spirit. As I developed the ability to 'read' other people I settled on using my clairvoyance to conduct aura readings. I would use colour pencils with an outline of the human body, and my clairvoyance to glean a whole gamut of information about the person I was reading for. Their energy would show me their personality, their health issues, what was going on for them and what was to come as well. I found these readings to be quite insightful for people and enjoyed doing them immensely.

When beginning to understanding the workings of your psychic abilities, it is important to first start with understanding universal energy. It is through this energy that all psychic communication transpires and emits from one soul to another, being in this world or beyond.

It's all about Energy

Let's cast our mind back to our high school science lessons and what we were taught about energy. We were taught that every object is made up of atoms and molecules (groups of atoms linked together). It is the structure and density of these molecules which determine whether that object is gas, liquid or solid. This includes the chair I'm sitting on while writing this for you, the coffee I'm also drinking, to each and every one of us including our souls and our bodies. We were also taught that energy doesn't die, it just changes form. Hence, water (liquid) becomes ice (solid) when its environment is changed to freezing temperatures or it evaporates through the air in water vapour (gas) before building in clouds to become water again as rain. I generally like to keep things plain and simple, so this is about as scientific as I will get. For those interested in more detail of a scientific nature balanced with the spiritual, may I recommend *"Hands of Light"* by *Barbara Ann Brennan*.

Bearing this in mind, it means that you and I are composed of atoms and molecules with varying structure and densities. Scientifically, we already know that our bodies contain water, and can even rejuvenate and heal itself. Now extend this belief to the existence of the Human Energy Field otherwise known as the Aura. Our aura, which houses the body comprises of more atoms and molecules which vibrate at a rate so fast that most people are not able to see this part of ourselves. This is the part of yourself you are now learning to connect and communicate with.

Science can also tell us that atoms and molecules can retain information. Much like a hydrogen atom contains information specific to hydrogen, and helps to identify who it is and its difference from other atoms, then so to do your atoms. Your aura and its atoms and molecules of energy can hold information pertinent to who you are. Put simply, your aura can hold all your feelings, emotions, experiences and infinite wisdom built up throughout your journey, including information detailing the health of our mind, body and soul. For example, the memory and emotion associated with my first day at school, or the intermittent neck pain I suffer with which I am yet to understand emotionally. Some say our energy even carries with it our past life information as well.

Mediumship development is a process of raising your awareness, so understanding your own energy is vitally important. As we gain knowledge of where our own energy ends and the energy of others begins, we begin looking at the world around us as a world of energy. This then enables us to gain an awareness of when our own energies are being touched or affected by another, including Spirit. It is in this state of awareness that we are then able to communicate in new energetic ways. However, it all begins with understanding ourselves first.

Exercise to feel energy

This exercise is very simple and designed for those of you, who are not experienced with working with the universal energies. For me this exercise always validates the existence of these unseen energies. Have fun with it and enjoy.

- Sit somewhere quiet where you will have a few minutes of undisturbed peace.
- Close your eyes and imagine a brilliant ray of sunshine pouring over you. So powerful, it warms you right through.
- Once you feel warm, bring your two hands together in front of you about 15cm apart.
- Imagine this ray of sunshine pouring out of each hand filling the space between your hands like a brilliant round ball of energy. A miniature sun if you will.
- You may find varying forms of reactions in your hands to the energy. Feelings such as warmth, tingles, cool breezes, heaviness or pressure, are some of the different ways each one of us feel the energy. I myself most commonly feel tingles.

- Once you have the yellow energy working in your hands, please spend a few minutes playing with your sun. Move your hands around to feel the difference when you manipulate the energy. Can you move them closer? What happens when you try to turn them in a clock wise direction or in an anti-clock wise direction?
- After spending a few minutes doing this, we are now going to change the colour of the energy ball. To do this, imagine that the brilliant sunshine has given way to a crisp blue day with a waterfall flowing over you.
- As this waterfall makes its way through your hands and into your ball of energy, pay attention to the subtle changes your ball will make. Does it change temperature? Does it feel heavier or lighter? Are you now feeling warmth, tingles, cool breezes, heaviness or pressure and is this different to before.

Tip: *You may want to keep practicing this exercise and change the colour, using all the rainbow colours or chakra colours. If you find certain colours easier than others to work with, this indicates an abundance of that colour in your aura. Colours you may struggle with can indicate a blockage in that auric layer and chakra.*

I hope you had fun with this exercise. For those of you that may be thinking *"I didn't feel anything"* please persist a few times ensuring you have the appropriate environment. Even try it with a friend. The more you practice, the more your awareness of the energies will increase and it will become easier to feel the subtle differences.

COMPOSITION OF THE HUMAN ENERGY FIELD

The aura is essentially a big ball of energy with your body as its centre. The aura houses the body, not the other way around. Remember vibrating atoms and molecules. It is influenced by how we feel, what we are thinking and what we are trying to manifest into our lives. Your health and vitality, your mental, emotional and spiritual health are all depicted in your aura. It is here that ailments can be detected, that depression can be felt and attachments to previous experiences can be carried. Therefore who we are in the moment has a direct influence on our aura.

The human energy field is predominately comprised of seven interchangeable layers, which all interrelate and are somewhat dependant on each other. Each layer is directly connected to one of the seven major energy vortexes, known as a chakra. As I see it, the chakra is part of the aura and the two cannot really be separated. Each chakra takes in universal energy and feeds the aura and subsequently the body with the life force of the Divine. Therefore the relationship between a chakra and its corresponding auric layer are so closely related that one would not exist without the other.

Colour comes to the aura by the vibrational frequency of the energy of each layer. For example, the energy of the physical auric layer vibrates on the colour spectrum at red. Each layer vibrates at a different range on the colour spectrum, thus resulting in the seven major colours and corresponding layers. Other colours are mixed in the aura much in the same way an artist would mix colour on his palette. The varying layers mix and interconnect with one another causing colour mixes like Red + Blue = Purple. However, there is so much more to this than a mixing of colour, for once you understand the meaning of each auric layer you'll understand that it is also a mixing of physical, emotional and spiritual meaning. For a simple example, Purple is the mixing of the Physical Auric layer (Red) and the Layer of Self Expression (Blue). Thereby, this example would represent the fact that this person would be working on expressing their spirituality in their day to day life.

Individual auras vary in strength, intensity and physical depth just as much as we individuals vary. An aura which is small, weak and unsettled by nature indicates someone who is unsure of themselves, or perhaps in ill health, while an aura which is strong and vibrant reflects someone who is sure of who they are and their place in this world. Our auras are such a reflection of who we are that the individual nature of the energy cannot be denied.

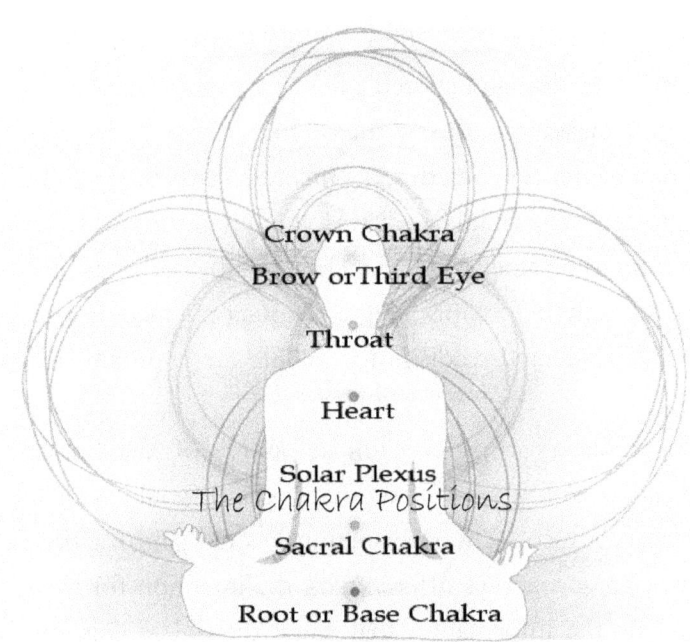

The Chakra Positions

SEEING AND FEELING THE AURA

Over the years, the most common question about auras I am asked is whether or not I can see auras. No, I generally cannot see them with my physical eyes, however I can see them clairvoyantly with my third eye. There are people who can physically see the human energy field, just like they see everything else around them, however I do believe this to be quite a rare experience. It is more common for people to have the occasional glimpse of seeing energy in this way, and using one's spiritual abilities to 'see', 'feel' and 'read' the aura. I believe everyone has the ability to be able to that.

Personally, there have only been a handful of times when I have physically seen someone's aura, and I find it easier to do if that person is a medium because of the heightened energy in their aura at the time. These experiences have ranged from seeing energy outlines of people's bodies, to glimpses of colour especially around their head and third eye, and to even seeing the outline of Spirit within a medium's auric field. I remember sitting in church a few years ago watching a medium giving out her messages and saw the outline of what I thought was a child. Not long after thinking this, the medium starts to say that she was beginning to feel very childlike. It was very interesting to watch. It is more common to be able to feel and clairvoyantly see auras. In fact, as I mentioned briefly before, prior to developing my mediumship ability this is how I conducted readings for people for approximately seven years.

Using a sheet of paper with an outline of the human body on it and along with a set of colour pencils, I would scan the aura using my clairvoyance. The information I could gain for people was often surprising and always offered with the intention for them to be empowered by the information that came through. This way, from whatever was uncovered, I could offer advice and tools for them to heal and change their life.

Eventually as my mediumship grew, I knew I needed to let go of offering these types of readings if I was to continue to grow with mediumship. I found at the time, with my mediumship in its early stages of development, my abilities didn't allow for both. These days, I can still do them, you never forget, although mostly I use the knowledge in spiritual healing and when teaching others about auras.

Should you go on to develop an interest in the human energy field, please remember my experience. It is common for people to place unrealistic expectations on themselves in regards to physically seeing the aura with their eyes only to be disappointed. If you do see them this way then great, that's a bonus. However it is more realistic for people to be able to connect with an aura using their psychic abilities. This is the goal to set yourself. Before we move on to a general overview of the auric layers and chakras here are a couple of exercises which will assist with seeing and feeling the aura.

Exercise to Feel the Aura

You will need a friend for this exercise.

- Have your friend stand a few feet away from you with their arms outstretched to the side. 5-6ft is a good starting point.
- Take another few steps away from your friend.
- Rub your hands together to stimulate your energies and raise them in front of you with palms out towards your friend.
- As you stand there, take note of any sensations you are feeling in your palms. Are you not feeling anything or is there a sensation of sorts at this point. Either is ok.
- Slowly taking one step at a time, walk towards your friend. Pay attention to when you start to sense a change on your palms. It is at this point that you are now connecting with the aura.
- Continue to move in closer to your friend, slowly stopping when your hands are just a few inches away.
- Keeping a few inches away from your friends' body, move your hands all over and around the outside of your friend noting any changes felt in the hand.

The last time I did this exercise, I found that I could feel a strong and confident aura if I was a few feet out and away from the persons body. This changed quite dramatically the closer I moved into her auric field and nearer the body, becoming weaker with a lack of confidence. When I shared this insight with the lady, she explained that her martial art training related to this. She had trained to keep people at an arm's length physically and she was quite confident in being able to do this. Personally, she shared how she is a little shy and growing into her confidence.

The sensations felt in the hands will be different for each person, but can range from tingles, heat or coolness. Some people may even experience slight discomfort. Any or all of these are great at this point. Another suggestion for this exercise is to do this once noting all that you feel, then to cleanse your friends aura with a smudge stick of sage and then try the exercise again. I would fully expect there to be a notable difference after the aura has been cleansed in this way.

A smudge stick is a bundle of dried herbs, usually white sage which is set alight and used to purify the energies associated with people and our environments. This practice heralds from the ancient Native American Shaman, and has been adopted worldwide by those conscious of energy and the positive impact this practice has. Being quite simple to do, for me the only important step to include is to ensure you conduct your ceremony in prayer with an intention to cleanse the energies of any negativity, releasing the energy that does not serve you. This in turn allows more love to flow into the energetic space, creating a whole new vibe.

Secondly, another good friend to practice this on is your family pet. Have fun with it, and if you add the intention of sending love and healing you are already well on your way to opening up as a Spiritual Healer.

Exercise to See the Aura

I have included this exercise because though I have explained it is not generally a realistic goal to achieve seeing the aura as a workable ability, I do know that most people want the opportunity to try anyway. Again just remember to have some fun. This reminds me of a time during the first group I ever taught, when one of the students brought in one of her daughter's hats because she could see her daughter's energy all around it. It was supposedly bright pink in nature, though I would never know. That night we all focused on the hat, with me, the teacher apparently being the only person who couldn't see it.

Again, you will need a partner for this exercise.
- Have your partner stand up against a white or plain light coloured wall.
- Ensure you have the best lighting possible.
- Sit yourself directly in front of your friend, at least 6ft away.
- Look at your friend and more specifically at their aura, so close and around the body.
- As you gaze at your friend's aura, try to relax your focus as if you are almost seeing past them.

In time you may notice a band of white energy, or what I call a band of "nothingness" just a couple of inches thick around the body. This band of "nothingness" is really something of course. It's part of the auric field and can sometimes appear similar to seeing the heat energy at the end of the road on a very hot day. This exercise will also work with your pets and any plants or trees. Remember they too have auric fields.

The Physical Auric Layer and Base Chakra

This layer is the layer usually found closest to the body and relates to the physical well being of the body and the physical energy reserves of the person. It is an energetic blue print of the physical body including all the anatomical parts and organs. This allows illness to be detected and healed here before it reaches the body.

All emotional issues having been held in any part of the aura will eventually make its way through this layer as they enter the body and become illness or ailments. This is the true purpose of this layer. Thus having a direct effect on the physical levels of energy and how we feel about our life.

People who live directed from this layer are very physical by nature. They are always doing, doing, doing, and not being able to stop. Their focus is all about what it is they are doing, and they are generally not comfortable focusing on emotional issues. So conversations with them would be about "*What did you do today……*" You won't find yourself talking to these people about how they feel emotionally.

Positively, a vibrant and healthy physical auric layer and base chakra speaks of someone who fully accepts life here on earth and approaches it with a 'can do' attitude. They will be hard workers, always striving to work towards a solution and often will not sit still for long. If you need something done, these are the people to call. Negatively they can be quick to anger and often miss what's really important by being emotionally detached.

Each layer has a related colour on the colour spectrum, which science tells us indicates the vibrational frequency of the energy within this layer. Red is the colour related to the physical auric layer which is in turn fed energy by the root or base chakra. This chakra is located over our pubic region or coccygeal centre.

Besides feeding energy to the aura, each chakra also feeds energy to certain bodily organs and glands. For the base chakra these are the adrenal glands, the spinal column, kidneys and urinary tracts.

In terms of the emotional and spiritual responsibility of the physical auric layer and the base chakra, it is here that all experiences we still hold relating to our earliest experiences can be found. From the point of conception, our early childhood through to our preteen existence will be stored here. It also supports how we feel about our place in this earthly world, and all that is required of us to maintain our physical needs here. In real terms, having experienced your parents separating at a very early age, any unresolved emotion associated with this experience will reside here. It was only last night while teaching a class around this chakra that Spirit showed me a little more information about myself in regards to this. During the meditation which was designed around the inner child and delivered so beautifully by Susanne, an experienced student who is making her foray into teaching, that I saw myself between the ages of 3 and 4. I gained a sense of the arguments my parents were experiencing at the time, and then knew that my father had left. Having loved him so much, I learnt that when he left and I didn't see him again, I very quickly shut down that emotion and disconnected from it out of self preservation. While still in the meditation, I then recognised that this is something I still do today, and quite easily when it comes to people leaving my life. Realising this gives me the power now to change and not shut down as I face the prospect of my best friend, Nicole moving away. Of course, Spirit always has impeccable timing.

The emotional or spiritual truth of how we feel about providing for our family and the struggles of maintaining our living in this world is in the physical auric layer. It is the energy of this layer which emotionally supports us getting out of bed every morning. Should there be any blockages felt in the aura at this layer, pay particular attention to where they are, as before too long that negative energy will turn into a physical ailment around where the current blockage exists. Remember this layer is an anatomical blueprint.

A blockage in the aura can be uncovered in many different ways, as we all will feel and experience the energy in different ways. One simple way to identify blockages is by hot spots, or a dramatic change in the energy as you feel your way around the aura with the exercise to 'Feel the Aura' above. In my early days of development, I would often use a crystal pendulum held over the chakras so I could see how the energy vortexes were flowing.

Key characteristics of physical/red energy:
- Warm
- Supportive and secure
- Strength
- Physically active disposition
- Task orientated
- Balance
- Agitation
- Anger
- Supportive of trance mediumship

With the writing of this book, I came to realise that I have also shut down and disconnected to a lot of emotions connected to my father leaving, and the effects of this have been indelible on my own soul. With this new insight I am now aware this is an area of my life that requires addressing and deep healing as I continue to work with what the physical auric layer and base chakra presents to me.

The Emotional Body and Sacral Chakra

So closely are the sacral chakra and the emotional body related, it's very hard to distinguish between the two different purposes when you are working with someone's aura. Located over the sacrum or just below the navel, the sacral chakra feeds energy to the prostate gland, ovaries and testicles, while energetically supporting the pelvic region and the reproductive organs.

This auric layer is the depositary for all things associated with our adolescence, our awakening sexuality and the realisation that we are to forge our own way in this world. With the groundwork of the physical auric layer and base chakra laid and developed, it is here that the seat of who we are begins to align with our place in the world. This is the essence of those formative teenage years.

Embracing your sexuality is a key component to having a healthy vibrant chakra and auric layer. Those of us that are living the true purpose of coming together sexually with another will experience a vibrant orange chakra and auric layer, with this energy manifesting in a healthy sexual libido and lifestyle in any relationship.

Blockages or any negative impacts on this energy will show in the aura as dull and lifeless in colour while feeling murky or clogged. These characteristics indicate an inhibited sexuality, while a maladjusted desire to satisfy ourselves by using our bodies will be seen by this layer feeling overstimulated and the orange being influenced with yellow.

Having this chakra function on its way to its full potential, will see an openness to yourself and others that didn't exist before. You become comfortable in who you are and know that the meaning of the true act of union is to value the other for all that they are, not to satisfy some basic physical need, like stress. Any deviation away from this reflects a dysfunction within this chakra. Your continued progress on your own path of self love will see this chakra improve naturally.

With our sexuality and how we relate to the opposite sex largely determined by our formative relationships, this layer is the storage keeper of our experiences long ago forgotten, especially regarding our more formative relationships. Ever wondered why people grow up to marry someone just like mum or dad? It's in the way the dynamics of such a mother/son or father/daughter relationship evolved in the formative years. Your relationship with your family unit has a reflection on all other relationships. Thus in this layer, we not only see sexual implications but also issues regarding those formative relationships.

People who have a dominance of orange in their aura have a great sense of freedom and creativeness. Easily bored they approach life with a sense of fun and excitement, and know that life is what you make it. This coupled with their strong sense of determination often sees them being successful in life and you'll generally find them with an active social life. People with a strong emotional body enjoy the connection of others and the socialness this can bring. Negatively, they can be self centred, whimsical and flighty, often with a total lack of direction. Driven by their past and often distracted by happiness outside of themselves, they can be childlike and attention seekers holding strong egos as a reflection of never completely moving past their adolescence.

Key characteristics of sacral/orange energy:
- Easily stimulated
- Unrestricted
- Healthy
- Creativity
- Excitement
- Determination
- Whimsical
- Flighty

The Mental Body and Solar Plexus Chakra

The energy of the mental body and the solar plexus chakra is a bright sunshine yellow and is there to support us in our effort to be true to ourselves. Being guided from this centre which holds the seat of our intuition is first and foremost the role the solar plexus chakra plays, while physically supporting the pancreas, stomach, liver, gall bladder, nervous and digestive systems with energy. It is here we find ourselves embracing our inner self or sitting in fear of it.

Many a time, I have seen a gifted student work hard to reveal their true spirit along with their developing spiritual abilities, only to come upon the challenge of the solar plexus and lose their way. The fear of self is something we all possess to varying degrees and as we walk a path guided by Spirit we are inevitability walking a path that guides us to reveal our true Spirit, that part of ourselves which is connected to the Divine, so it becomes the most dominant aspect of who we are. This journey has us constantly seeing ourselves in a new light, as we grow to love ourselves more and challenge those aspects of ourselves which are not so great. Going through this we notice ourselves letting go of old beliefs as new ones start to take hold, and we find ourselves thinking differently. Not only about ourselves but the world around us, as we come to a new acceptance of who we are. As a result of this journey, our life starts to change and manifest in ways we often do not expect, and for some people this can be difficult to confront. We start to realise the truth in the life we have been living and begin to see that there are areas of our life that need healing and changing. These areas can be difficult to face as these changes impact our relationships, our home life, our friendships and our careers, all of which can be challenging areas to transition change. Being true to who you are though, is a great gift and brings with it a wonderful sense of freedom.

Located in the centre region of our torso just at the bottom of the rib cage, a balanced solar plexus chakra and mental body of the aura will have a good dose of yellow in their aura. They will have a great mental capacity and can quickly understand how to approach things with practicality. They enjoy being challenged and are fun to be around as their sunny, positive disposition easily rubs off on you.

Negatively they can tend to over analyse everything and lead a life from the head a little too much, which easily leads to bouts of confusion. Imbalances in the energy here usually results in one of two directions. Too much energy will see an over stimulation leading to an ego centered mentality where it becomes 'all about me' and 'I am better than others' while a lack of energy results in an underplayed manner identifying someone having a distinct lack of self esteem and believing they are not worthy.

This has been a big challenge for me over the years to see myself as being worthy and allowing my true spirit to shine through with confidence, and in so doing, letting go of the fear of being ridiculed and worrying about how other people might judge me. I have come to understand that my spirit guides have played a large role in that journey with each of them representing a different aspect of my true self. With hindsight I see this now, as a spirit guide means so much more than a being a messenger from Spirit. Their true role is to reveal yourself to you in a way that gently guides you through that process.

For me it has been my guide White Feather who has culminated that learning for me. We originally met in 2005 as I was just coming out of a very challenging time. My mum had just been through major heart surgery with a triple heart bypass and at the same time my marriage was falling apart. Over the years I had changed from the young twenty one year old my husband Rod had married, who only needed support on a physical level. My emotional support came from myself or my girlfriends, having learnt early on in childhood that there was only me to rely on for that. At twentyone my spiritual self was not really a consideration, as I didn't really understand that side of me existed. As I grew older and found spiritualism and my mediumship I certainly needed more from my partner. No longer was I happy to have the seemingly separate lives and friends, only coming together to parent and provide for the family. I now needed a partner who was more willing to share my journey. I am glad to say that although we were presented with a tough challenge, with some counselling and the willingness of my husband to not only accept the new me, but to also embrace his own growth and change, we are still together with our new relationship stronger and better than it has ever been.

White Feather entered just as all this was nearing completion. It was her that helped me to see the purpose behind all of this learning. I needed to be more secure in who I had become and more accepting of all that I truly deserve. She needed me to see all this before she could reveal her true plans. For it was White Feather who inspired me to step out more with my mediumship and establish The Australian College of

Mediumship.

However, it has only been as recent as this week, while living consciously with the energy to write this section on the solar plexus chakra and the mental auric body that I fully stepped into the true me. We can laugh a little at what a slow learner I am.

Having come home from teaching class one Wednesday night, as I lay in bed trying to drift off to sleep, in my clairvoyant mind I was approached by a native american male indian who was sitting around a camp fire. He said to me "You do know that White Feather is your true self, don't you?" As I replied that I did, I saw her walk into view and become one with me. We then joined in the proceedings around the camp fire as I was shown that the next six months of my life were about getting comfortable and living a life even more attuned to who I truly am and the life I truly deserve. The creative energy that supports this is clear, free of the fear of self and therefore knows no boundaries. While this is a fairly significant shift in my belief of who I am, I'm sure it won't be the last. Journeys such as this are a lot like peeling away the layers of an onion, including the crying.

Key characteristics of solar plexus/yellow energy:
- Happy and joyful
- Warmth
- At one with self or lack of self identity
- Bursting with joy
- Stabilising
- Over analysing and confusion
- Enjoys a challenge
- Preparedness for what is to come
- Clouded energy

The Layer of Love and Heart Chakra

Love is the centre of all things living, so it stands to reason that the centre of our energy field is based in love as well. It is through our heart centre that we express who we are in the light of love. It is here where we process how we feel about others and the world at large, which then often has us respond to people and situations as we do. Through the art of self love, we can see the truth of another reflected in our own heart. Acknowledging that truth is the difficult part, as this then becomes our own reflection while we work towards seeing and learning our old tired and broken behaviour patterns in our relationships and our interactions with others. Forming a basis of the energy, one should lay as a foundation for living a life based in guidance, this is a key component in your ability to be 'at one' with the Universe.

The heart chakra and its associated layer of love connect the higher spiritual chakras with that of the lower physical ones creating a balance and connectedness between your spiritual self and how that relates to your everyday life. When connected through all the other energy centres, this love transforms into Divine Love making us aware of the Divine presence in all creation and guides us to unity with all in the Universe. On its way to achieving this, our heart must learn to love and forgive, to understand and accept.

The heart chakra is energetically responsible for the thymus gland, the heart, blood, vagus nerve and circulatory system. Located in the centre of the chest, it is often the most inhibited and the hardest chakra for us to allow to reach its full potential. Coupled with the auric layer of love, the heart chakra will permeate through the universe how much unconditional love you walk with. Unfortunately, because we feel we are at times vulnerable to easily being hurt, it is most often partially closed off to protect oneself from such hurts. Opening ourselves up to guide our lives by how we feel is the only key you need, along with a good dose of courage.

Identified by the colour green, people with this colour or the layer of love dominating their energy, will be people who tend to wear their heart on their sleeve. However, it is quite possible they have become very adept at protecting themselves. It is rare to see the full expression of this layer in the aura. Most often, we see parcels here and there placed throughout the aura depicting where this person is healing and working at bringing more love into their existence.

It's also an extremely important part of the aura, for those developing their spiritual gifts. A spirit guide once said *"For to see clairvoyantly, is to see with your heart."* This means that a large part of opening yourself to your spiritual gifts means opening your heart. My own personal experience has proven that this is true in the strongest sense of the word and a journey that is never ending.

When you live a heart centred life you are in tune with your purpose, feel in touch with nature and have a love and compassion for all of mankind. For me, when this energy is at its full potential it feels like I am working with Jesus. His energy shows me the potential of humanness that you and I can aspire to be. Full of unconditional love, bearing no judgements, an ability to forgive beyond measure and a level of faith and trust in his place in the universe that most of us only dream about. While I'm not sure that I personally can achieve this in this lifetime, it is a vision I work towards along my journey of love and evolution.

Key characteristics of heart/green energy:
- Freedom or restriction
- Seeing truth in others
- Past and current relationships
- Being in tune with one's purpose
- Soulmate connections linked to your purpose
- Blending with nature
- Love for all mankind

- Sadness
- Envy and hollowness

The Layer of Self Expression and Throat Chakra

Widely recognised as the chakra associated with communication, I believe its responsibilities reach far deeper than that as the auric layer of self expression merges with the throat chakra to provide an energy system that is designed to support you in your efforts to express to the world who you truly are. Do you fully express your thoughts and wants, or do you reserve these out of fear and therefore inhibit yourself.

Bring forth that which resides within you from the thoughts, the feelings to the intricate nature of who you want to be and how you wish to live. Leave no stone unturned as you find it within yourself to live this way. Developing a greater sense of self will find you improving this which often leads to life changes as people reach understandings of themselves.

Living the positive expression of this energy will see an abundance of blue within the aura. Such a person has a great sense of a peaceful freedom to be who they want to be, often having great clarity and a clear sense of direction. They will have a willingness to let go and learn from others and will be quite insightful. There is an easy level of acceptance of their self and others as their self assurity runs deep like a river.

It is important to understand that this chakra and its auric layer have an intricate relationship with our ego, with our ego being that aspect of ourselves which resides in fear, doubt and negativity. Expressing our selves based in these emotions or taking action rooted in these same fear based behaviours transpires through this body of energy diminishing its strength, vitality and creating blocks within the chakra.

Encountering dull, lifeless energy in the region of a particular organ can indicate which aspect of the self is being inhibited and/or has the ego driving its expression. As a child and living with as much fear I did, at the time caused me to withdraw and become more of a loner. Not knowing any better, I played into this and continued to sit with that energy for many years which resulted in regular bouts of lethargy, sore throats, cold sores and flu like symptoms. At least once a year I would encounter a winter flu severe enough to need rest and days away from school or work. It was easier for me to wallow in such sickness. One of the first changes I noticed as I attuned more spiritually was the end of this ill health. No longer did I entertain a yearly visit of influenza. This pattern of ill health had no place in my new energy and while I still will occasionally come down with a cold or mild flu, the severity is not as it was nor is the regularity of it. Colds and flu are quite common if this layer is depleted of energy as the organs which are supported with energy here are the bronchial and vocal apparatus, the lungs and alimentary canal while the gland supported is the thyroid.

It is with forethought and understanding that will lead to opening this chakra to its full potential. Take time between your thoughts and expressing them out loud. Much needed thoughts and words are often left unexpressed which leaves the world without your much needed wisdom. Take time to ensure that your response to others or the behaviour you exhibit are all connected to that part of you which is connected to love and understanding. Even try to gain an understanding of which part of you is making your decisions. In time, we come to new levels of accepting who we truly are and therefore are even more prepared to share ourselves with others.

Key characteristics of throat/blue energy:
- Willingness to let go of harm to others
- Insightful expression
- Impatience
- Coolness
- Acceptance

- Listening from the heart
- Peaceful
- Freedom to be who you want to be
- It is through self expression that one's ego is maintained

The Intuitive Plane and the Brow Chakra

The energy created by these two aspects of our aura define our perception and how we see the world. Do we see through the eyes of ego and judgement or do we see from a deeper part of ourselves more closely connected with our hearts.

Intricately connected to our spiritual abilities of clairvoyance, clairaudience and clairsentience this layer of the aura and its corresponding third eye chakra has a direct impact on the functioning of these abilities. With higher awareness and living a life that is sourced from a deeper part of who we are will see this energy clear and be fully functional, inspiring deeper insight for you and those around you. However, come from a place of ego and judgement with a mind full of doubt and negativity, and you'll see this auric layer spiral into repetition and cloudiness.

Like I mentioned earlier, *"to see clairvoyantly is to see with your heart."* This epitomises the way in which to reach the full potential of this layer of your aura. Anything else diminishes its power, leading to clouded thought and clouded judgement. With this said it is easy to understand then how someone who has their aura consisting of a vibrant indigo colour will be a clear thinker and lead a life with a clear direction.

With this chakra located in the middle of the forehead it reminds us of the importance for the mind to be in tune with the heart for all seeing wisdom to flow through your life. This ability allows us to see beyond what is being presented before you. To see beyond the surface and gain greater insight into the circumstances and people who come across your path. This awareness then connects directly to our intuition leading us forward to a life with purpose.

Imbalances in these areas affect our abilities to see ourselves with truth. Often leading us to blame others for mishaps and misappropriations, which are genuinely brought about through co-creation for our own highest good. Over time many individuals even develop blindness to such matters. Even those professing to live with awareness can be guilty of such indiscretions from time to time. Ask yourself?

I recall gaining some insight during one of my courses a few years ago. This course was called Understanding Energy and covers the chakras and auric layers in some detail. Each fortnight we would cover a different body of energy and its relevant chakra. As the teacher, it is common for Spirit to work with me through my life experiences, helping me to gain new insights and understandings relevant to subject matter I might be teaching while also guiding me to apply it in my life. With this particular class we were about to cover the brow chakra. In the lead up to that class, I had been experiencing a lot of judgement directed my way by some of the students and in other work related areas. It is in my nature to look within, so I began that process by being honest and seeing how I too may have been passing judgement and letting go of these thoughts. It was a huge fortnight with a lot of self healing brought about, however it wasn't until preparing for the brow chakra class that I and Nicole, one of the ACOM teachers at the time, had the realisation that what we were experiencing was directly connected to this class and was brought about by the energy of the third eye chakra and the intuitive plane. While I knew that Spirit's way is to teach through experience, I sometimes can be a bit slow on the up take. We laughed even harder when we finally realised it had been happening all the way along and it took us until the sixth chakra to get it. Lucky Spirit has a lot of patience.

Associated with the pituitary gland, the lower brain, eyes, ears, nose and nervous system, this chakra is of a very high frequency with a very fine and sensitive nature. It is therefore easily affected by the other layers. The clearer and more attuned all the lower bodies are, the easier it is to work with this layer and what it has to offer, namely the spiritual gifts. This is one of the main reasons children experience psychic happenings so easily. The highest potential for this chakra and auric layer is for you to live from a space of inner awareness and guidance, seeking only to come from within.

Key characteristics of third eye/indigo energy:
- Clarity of judgement
- Clear thinking
- At one with ego self
- All seeing wisdom
- Seeing truth in situations

The Godself connection and the Crown Chakra

While the crown chakra is often quoted as being the centre for Divine connection, in truth it is only one aspect of such a connection. All be it, a very important one. Personally from an energetic healing perspective, I believe that this chakra and its corresponding layer does not ever require an energetic healer to work on it for the purpose of clearing a blockage. Yes this chakra has differing amounts of energy and therefore potential, however its functionality directly relates to the coming together of all the other energy centers and lower auric bodies. You see, a Divine connection comes from all the chakras working harmoniously together. For most of us we feel this and an increase in the energy of this center when we receive a new understanding or moment of enlightenment.

There are times in one's life that a moment of simplicity results in a moment of magic and profound change, as all the hard work you have put in finally comes together. In 2008 during one of our many visits to the US, my husband Rod and I visited the town of Sedona which is a couple of hours north of Phoenix, Arizona and is in the heart of Red Rock country. It is sacred land for many ancient native american tribes, among them the Sinaqua and Hohokam with archaeological evidence dating as far back as 8000BC. Currently there is a thriving metaphysical community, as many, many people find themselves not only drawn to its magnificent beauty but also to the Sedona healing energies for which it is widely known for.

Sedona is reputed to be a world vortex site, where the Earth's energetic ley lines meet, thus creating a zone of powerful, majestic energies much like Stonehenge in England, Machu Picchu in Peru, the Great Pyramids in Egypt and Australia's own Uluru.

Visiting Sedona was not initially part of the plan, as to be honest I was completely unaware of its spiritual reputation. However, Spirit certainly had other plans and leading up to the trip I began encountering a great deal of synchronistic events or coincidences, if you will, regarding Sedona. From people talking to me about Sedona to quite a few travel shows appearing on TV just at the right time. Being someone who not only believes in synchronicity, but lives my life consciously being guided by them, I knew that Sedona was a must to visit.

The drive to Sedona was uneventful, although my expectations were high as my intuition had been telling me something special was to take place specifically with regards to how I would feel. Even so, what unfolded still completely took me by surprise.

Our first stop was at Montezuma's Castle, which is the ancient remains of native cliff dwellers and is about half an hour from Sedona. Following this, we moved to the Chapel of the Holy Cross, which gives you a panoramic view of all of Sedona's Red Rock formations and their corresponding vortex sites, a breathtaking view in itself. Alighting from the tour van and coming in physical contact with the land resulted in

Old Cherokee Wisdom

One evening an old Cherokee Indian told his grandson about a battle that goes on inside people.

He said *"My son, the battle is between two 'wolves' inside us all. One is Evil. It is anger, envy, jealousy, sorrow, regret, greed, arrogance, self-pity, guilt, resentment, inferiority, lies, false pride, superiority, and ego.*

The other is good. It is joy, peace, love, hope, serenity, humility, kindness, benevolence, empathy, generosity, truth, compassion and faith."

The grandson thought about it for a minute and then asked his grandfather: *"Which wolf wins?"*

The old Cherokee simply replied *"The one you feed."*

Author Unknown.

this overwhelming feeling of having 'come home'. This feeling erupted throughout my entire being, right to my very core. There was such a sense of peace and completion that I became quite emotional. Had I been here before? Not in this life time. Was this a past life connection?

As is my nature, I couldn't help myself but to immediately try to come to some understanding of what was happening. So firstly, I entered the Chapel questioning if it was the church I felt connected to. No. After lots of photo taking we made our way into town, so still questioning, I was asking myself *"Is it the town I feel connected to?"* No. This was all confirming for me, that it was truly the land that I felt connected to.

In time I was told it was my *'Spiritual Home'*. As grateful for this insight as I was, it then presented a new question. *What does that really mean?* Was it the place itself or was it the powerful energies providing a healing release bringing me closer to our true home, the world of Spirit, like I have never experienced before? Somehow I sense that it is a combination of both, which only a return visit will provide more insight and understanding to.

Certainly the experience itself was something for my history books, however, the lasting effects on me personally have been the most intriguing. Since that moment at the Chapel of the Holy Cross, I feel like a new person and the only way I can describe it is to use the old Cherokee parable of the two wolves. This parable speaks of an internal struggle we all have, where our Spirit is constantly challenged by our Ego. Well, that struggle was very true for me.

Over the years I have constantly worked with awareness to live from my spirit and not allow my ego self to rule with its self doubt, judgements and lack of love. This at times has regularly felt like hard work and a constant struggle, although until Sedona I was really unaware of how much of a struggle it truly was.

Since that very moment, the struggle no longer exists in the same way. No longer is it a daily battle going on within. My sense of Self is much stronger, my Spirit is at the forefront and easily accessible, with the self doubt being a much smaller part of my every day internal dialogue. My ego self still exists, however, I now find it to be less powerful and more manageable as if it knows its place. As myself doubt rises, not only is it a lot less often but it feels like I am detached from it in some way. The thoughts are at a distance as I readily remind myself that they are part of the old Kerrie and the new Kerrie can quickly switch that around and return to love.

My understanding of this change within is twofold. Firstly, the energies of Sedona sparked a profound healing and release cementing in place all the self healing I had worked on over the years. This brought about a feeling of being whole as I'd never felt before. I believe up to this point, my soul had been fragmented and disconnected in many ways I may never fully understand. Certainly I believe, that our hurts can accumulate and disconnect us from others, from ourselves and from the Divine.

Over the years I have had many experiences of self healing and gaining new understandings of who I am as I consistently worked on filling those holes in my soul, whether I was aware of them or not. However, not until such an experience can you fully comprehend the effect of this kind of separation and the effect it has on who we are and our birthright to be completely connected to our Creator.

Had I visited last year or before, or had I not worked on myself in the way I have over the years, would my visit to Sedona have provoked this magnificent healing release? I think not. It is my understanding that my experience in Sedona is not an isolated case; actually I suspect it could be quite common. It is God's way, leading you to a moment in time where you can unfold your capacity to bring about your own healing. Do you need to visit a place like Sedona to achieve that? No, I don't think so, but it sure makes it so much more spectacular.

This experience encapsulates how when the timing is right, the crown chakra and energy of the Godself connection can bring about a greater divine you, through your connection to the Divine light of love. Living from this energy plane brings about the manifestation of living a life from the light.

The associated colour is violet, so a person with this layer open and working positively will have a predominance of violet in there aura and will knowingly understand the essence of creating with the Universal energies and is able to use them consciously to shape their reality, knowing they are responsible in this co-creation process. Deterring from this knowing, forces this chakra to detract from itself, forcing it to withhold the light of energy to pass through to the rest of the being and corresponding energy bodies. This, I believe is the only imbalance that can occur here. To be of the light or not. To embrace love or not. To live a life from love or not. This chakra is also energetically responsible for the pineal gland and the upper brain and right eye.

My Higher Self says:
"Divinity is but the compilation of all the energy centres and auric layers coming together as one, seeking your connection to the world around you. Knowing your place in the universe and understanding you, are but one of God's creatures in this great garden of Eden."

Key characteristics of crown/violet energy:
- A knowingness that we are all connected as one and a part of the divine matrix
- An understanding that we are soul first and human second with a driving force to know that is truth
- Bliss
- Completeness
- Wondrous love

- Spinning, dizziness represents a disconnection here

The last two layers are strongly dependant on the life force and connections of the other layers. For example - being consciously aware of your energy and nurturing your lower bodies will allow a closer connection to these two planes. The blending of the frequencies is more easily achieved and therefore the results you need to come from these parts of you will happen more effectively.

Exercise to experience and feel colour

There is one last exercise I'd like to share with you regarding feeling energy. This exercise is designed to help you feel the characteristics of colour in the energy and will help you to expand upon what I have offered here. I remember the first time I ever conducted this exercise in a class. It was certainly an eye opener and lots of fun, especially when we came across the energy of orange and its sexual characteristics. To me it felt very attuned to the Hippy movement of the 1960's and the association of free love and all that that era encompassed. We enjoyed it so much that orange became a code word for those in the know and just a way for us to have a laugh.

- This exercise can be conducted by yourself, however you may yield better results from working with a group.
- Begin with a meditation to center and balance your energies.
- At the conclusion of the meditation, bring your awareness into the room and become aware of your body - however try to maintain the quiet and relaxed feel.
- In your own time ask for a white light of energy to pour through the roof and into your circle, embracing you and wrapping itself around you like a blanket.
- As it does this, pay attention to how it feels and what words spring

- to mind and voice them out loud. It may be beneficial to have an audio recorder nearby so you then have a record of your findings.
- Once you feel you have exhausted the characteristics of white, move onto another colour by asking for your chosen colour to come pouring into the room in the same way as you did with white. I suggest completing this for all the colours of the rainbow at the very least.
- You will also find that each colour will comprise of positive attributes as well as negative ones.

I'm a big believer that while you can easily find a lot of this type of information in books, this is other peoples wisdom and we always want to strive to develop our own. Experiencing your own beliefs and understandings in ways such as this exercise provides, does cement much stronger spiritual foundations for you. So please experiment with energy, work towards gaining an understanding and get to know how it feels for you. Learn to identify when it changes and bring home the understanding that all of life is created and sourced with the life force that is energy. Knowing this as a way of life, will stand you strong for future growth and ongoing development.

Protection and Grounding

It is relevant at this point that we talk a little about energetic protection and the process of grounding. Grounding enables us to balance our higher spiritually focussed energies with that of our lower physical energies. Imagine yourself being in the spirit world each and every time you make a connection. Doing this we often leave a part of ourselves behind, which over time can build up and impact us detrimentally, if your energies are not supposed to be there at the present time.

We can experience effects such as light headedness, loss of

thought and clarity where we find it hard to focus. Your disposed energies will also equate to unsteadiness, clumsiness and a feeling of not belonging or disconnectedness. Many times over the years I have needed to consciously work at grounding myself. Most times I am quite able to easily achieve this, though I find ensuring it is part of your everyday spiritual rituals has the greatest impact. It is really a case of prevention is better than cure.

What to look for when grounding is required
- Light-headedness
- Moodiness
- Failure to concentrate and think clearly
- Clumsiness
- Lack of sleep
- Feeling disconnected from everyone and everyone around you

Visualisation procedure for grounding
1. Place your feet flat on the floor
2. Imagine tree roots growing out of the soles of your feet, growing and securing themselves into mother earth, the ground beneath your feet. Quite simple, yet extremely effective.

I recommend that you ground yourself at the completion of any activity which involves you connecting with the spirit world, at the end of every meditation, when you have finished partaking in any form of spiritual healing, at the end of doing a reading and especially when you are new to psychic development and have finished any form of psychic exercise. I also think the necessary grounding process gives us an opportunity to be grateful for the connections to Spirit we have just made. So offering a prayer of thanks and gratitude during your visualisation is a good practice to develop.

A second visualisation you may like to use especially for group energies is to imagine standing in the centre of a lotus blossom which is drawing all the excess energy from around you. Be sure to feel it all drain away from around your body parts starting with the top of your head, working your way down to your toes.

Other Grounding tips
- Have a shower or bath.
- Go without shoes, especially walking on the grass or the beach.
- Housework and or gardening often have the same affect.
- Swimming.
- Getting back to nature.

Now this leads us to the practice of energetic protection. A popular practice in the spiritual and new age communities is where one visualises a shield of energy to protect their own energy from negativity and harm, be it from other people or the Spirit world.

I'm not a fan of this practice, I learnt a long time ago that if you feel the need for protection, then beyond that request you are holding a fear in some way. Band aiding or masking your fear with protection is not a sustainable answer, nor will it lay strong foundations in who you are. Certainly, the act of protection is real because of your intention and belief, however it keeps us in a victim mentality and really only serves to blame something or someone outside of ourselves for what happens to us and our energies.

I much prefer to approach this with personal responsibility, looking within and the belief that nothing can affect my energies unless I allow it to in some way. For example, I hear common discussions about people protecting their energies from psychic attacks (specifically directed negative thought forms with animosity) or psychic vampires (people who drain your energy). Most often, people are not even aware that they are affecting you in this way, yet we see it as their fault. Though if we took a moment to see ourself in this situation we would realise we are too trusting, too giving, too empathic, have soft boundaries and find it hard to say "*No*". How about changing some of this from within. Approaching it in this way has much longer lasting effects and sees our light grow much stronger providing a natural form of protection.

My Higher self explains this way:
"For a moment imagine, if you will, a light standing in the center of a room. This light attracts all sorts of bugs, dust particles and anything else that may come along. So too does the light we walk with. Our job is to ensure that our inner light is strong and radiant, filled with love which attracts and inspires others of the same ilk. Leaving our light encloaked in a shield which is not of your own inner making causes infirm and unstable foundations. Protection is not needed but truth is. Honour that you have some fear, honour that your mind holds negativity but you are working on it. Honour that you are not just yet where you want to be with your life, thoughts and beliefs but you know you'll get there. Walk in this light and it will be protection enough."

Over the years I have worked with many energies in Spirit which some would label as negative, malevolent, or from the lower astral (explained further in chapter six). However, not once have they been able to affect me negatively. If anything, I have gained great spiritual gifts and growth from working with them. One of my favourites was John Lynch, an energy associated with Berrima Courthouse in NSW whom I first met in 2006. John was charged, convicted and hung for ten murders in 1842 and is widely known as Australia's first serial killer.

I first came in contact with Berrima Courthouse and John after being guided to take the students currently sitting at ACOM on a ghost tour, to expose them and their Mediumship to energies beyond that of the class room environment. I never expected to be opening such a Pandora's box though. As is often the case with Spirit, you are lead on

It's all about Energy

a journey which is full of surprises with the outcomes tending to exceed your expectations. This was the case here.

After that first ghost tour and the ensuing months, John would regularly join us in class making himself known by approaching many of the students. His tell tale sign often resulted in them feeling physically ill. You might question what the purpose of this was and you would be right to do so. In fact, I hope you would question something of this nature with any spiritual practitioner.

I believe that who I am and my work is based in love, truth and healing. This coupled with the belief of the universal law that like attracts like, I know that on some level of John's soul he was ready to heal, find more love and evolve in some way. While he may not on the surface present in this way, as people do say and do things to disguise their truth, I trusted in this and my guides at the time.

I also knew that I and the ACOM community would all learn and grow from this teaching opportunity. And we did! John helped many to understand judgement and especially how we even apply it to the spirit world. He helped others to identify and understand the fear they had around working with Spirit. It was the feeling of nausea and illness which highlighted this. And for me, I learnt to stand strong in my own beliefs even though they can be different from conventional viewpoints. I did lose students who were uncomfortable and people did question why I was entertaining an energy that was a "low-level" entity and not from the "highest and best". Well, who are we to make that judgement. If love is all there is, then isn't that in there somewhere too. All I know, is that through working together we all learnt and evolved a little more and that's the "highest and best" intention for me.

Protection is a very personal issue and one we all have the right to decide whether we opt to use or not. While I never ask for protection from the Spirit world, I do occasionally use it in environments where my own physical energies can be affected. For example, visiting a hospital, shopping center or crowded event. Here I would visually work at containing my own auric field and acknowledge releasing any energy that does not work positively for me. In a hospital however, I would work more consciously with allowing my auric field to give out healing energy so long as I'm not drastically physically impacted on. All this is achieved just through prayer and visualisation. I would also certainly recommend using a form of protection for those who practice energetic healing and are strong in their empathy, especially if finding themselves easily taking on other people's concerns and emotions. I would do so though, while consciously working towards employing more natural boundaries which means changing some aspects within, like learning to say "*No*".

When engaging in the practice of energetic protection, please do so with a level of honesty with yourself, and over time taking some responsibility in working through why you feel the need for protection in the first place.

In this chapter:
- Energy doesn't die, it changes form.
- Try the simple yet powerful exercise to feel energy, adding your own colour changes to feel and experiment with.
- It is more common to 'see' the aura clairvoyantly than to 'see' physically with your own eyes.
- You can do exercises to develop your ability to feel auras with people and pets, plants, trees…
- Smudging is an efficient energy cleanser for both people and your environment like your home, office and workspace.
- The human energy field and its composition is explained including the seven chakras, the different ways they present and what their energies and characteristics mean.
- How does the old Cherokee parable about the two wolves apply to you? Can you relate to it and see its wisdom in parts of your life?

- Grounding is a vital aspect of all spiritual work with many ways to achieve this – work out what method works best for you.

Reaching your Highest Potential

> *Our deepest fear is not that we are inadequate.*
> *Our deepest fear is that we are powerful beyond measure.*
> **~Marianne Williamson.**

Unlocking your spiritual abilities can be likened to developing any other talent which lies within, that requires special attention to reach its full potential. Much like a yogi master has to study the art of spiritual evolvement and enlightenment or a musician who spends many hours in rehearsal or the artist who studies art and colour technique; we endeavour to unlock within us the power to receive information flowing through the universal super highway.

Please allow me to use this highway analogy to best describe how it is for each of us. The universal super highway is extremely busy, composed of many different energies (cars), many different highways leading to a variety of destinations (different levels of consciousness and awareness). Unravelling this mystery presents one with many connotations of how your car gets to its first destination. Some will travel route A, others route B, C , D or even Highway 51.

Along the way, you will encounter beautiful scenery, some straight roads as well as long winding ones. You will come across some places to stop and rest, while some of you may even encounter a little car trouble along the way. One thing for sure though, commencing this journey from point A, will unfold many unexpected events along your route and while you may think you have a destination in mind, I can assure you that as long as you follow the road signs along the way, you will end up in a destination which will take you by complete surprise and fill you with a sense of purpose that knows no bounds. However, to take such a journey, we first should attend to our car, ensuring that the oil and water are ok, with the engine tuned and the tyres fresh and ready, so that we are as prepared as we can be.

One of the first mistakes most people make when embarking on such a journey is comparing themselves to others. I have seen many, many people unrealistically compare their own abilities with those of well known mediums like John Edward, Gordon Smith or Lisa Williams. It is especially common for people to compare themselves with others in their own development circles. While doing this is human nature and I too have been guilty of this, it is flawed from the outset and really only serves to nurture our own self doubt and keep our confidence down. Instead, know that we all have our own strengths and weaknesses, and what may be a strength for one may be a challenge for another. As humans we all learn and express ourselves quite differently. Some of you may be quite visual by nature and find yourself quite talented in this area already. Do you have extremely visual dreams? Do you tend to notice colour and detail quite easily? Do you use words such as *"I see"* or phrases like *"Did you see…"*? If so then I suspect that your attention to the visual aspects of life are quite attuned. Therefore, it is likely that you'll find clairvoyance a strength.

Perhaps you tend to focus quite easily on the world of sound. Can you hear sounds before you see where they are coming from? In conversation do you find yourself intently focused on what your friend is saying as opposed to daydreaming at the same time (like me…)? Can you easily hear the layering in music? Do you use words such as *"I heard…."* or phrases like *"Did you hear…"* These all indicate a strong auditory nature, and should transfer to a strong clairaudient ability.

Lastly, are you quite a sensitive person who feels emotional or upset quite easily. Sympathetic to those around you and the world as a whole, while noticing easily how others feel. Do you express yourself easily with affection? A little touchy feely as I like to say. Do you use words such as *"I feel…"*? This all indicates a sentient nature which should transfer to your clairsentient ability being a strength.

To help you identify which style of learning and expression you may be, here is a simple Visual-Auditory-Kinaesthetic questionnaire.

Step 1: For each question select 1 option only.

	Visual	**Auditory**	**Kinaesthetic/ Touchy- Feely**
When learning something new for the first time, I prefer to:	Read the instructions	Listen to or ask for an explanation	Have a go and learn by 'trial & error'
To navigate while driving, I prefer to:	Read a map	Ask for directions	Follow my intuition
When speaking with people I use the words:	*"I see.."*	*"I hear…"*	*"I feel…"*

I remember things best by:	Writing notes	Saying things out loud	Doing
Most of my spare time is spent:	Watching television or movies	Talking with friends and family	Doing activities
I generally feel connected to people because of:	How they look	What they say to me	How they make me feel
It is easier for me to remember:	Faces	Names	Things I have done
Total:			

Step 2: Total your tally.

The category with the highest tally indicates your most common form of learning and expression. These basic human learning styles are the basis from which you will develop your spiritual abilities of clairvoyance, clairaudience and clairsentience.

At first you may encounter that one of your spiritual abilities is initially stronger than the others. This is how it should be. It takes time to develop all three abilities so they are equally functional. And as each of us are travelling different highways using different vehicles, how this unfolds will be different for each of us. So to compare what you may be clairvoyantly seeing with what someone else is experiencing is not beneficial nor is it an accurate way to see your own progress.

It is however quite rewarding and extremely beneficial to find ways to benchmark your own individual progress. In fact, it is something I recommend for you to do and to start now. To do this, first start with using a journal. Write each and every experience in your journal. Start with keeping track of your dreams, writing what happens when you are working through any of the development exercises. It helps to write down any thoughts, inspirations and anything else you perceive to be a message. From this you will be keeping track of your own development and will be able to see how far you've come from week to week, month to month or even year to year. I found this to be extremely helpful with increasing my confidence as I noticed not only the changes within myself, but also my predictive messages manifesting.

I was learning at a time before Australia had discovered John Edward and Crossing Over, so for the first seven years of my psychic development I was developing psychic awareness. My mediumship development was to come much later. Psychic awareness is focussed on the energies of this world and with a purpose of assisting others in understanding their life more and usually includes making future predictions. To gain a measure of one's accuracy, time would need to pass to see how my predictions faired. Hence, having my journal helped me to keep a record of my ability to receive messages. I found that during this time, my trust in myself was building and certainly highlighted for me, spiritually, how much doubt I walked with. This then allowed my guides to see and gain a better understanding of what was needed for my growth.

It is important to trust in yourself and your own abilities. Try to work towards never doubting what you are receiving, even if it doesn't make any sense. Actually, especially if it doesn't make any sense, as this certainly means you didn't make it up. The brain works so logically that something would have to make sense for you to make it up. Not trusting in the messages you receive will actually slow your progress and creates blockages in the energy, a bit like a radio receiver not in full working capacity and therefore not receiving all of the information. I'm sure you will find that part of your personal journey will be to increase your self belief and decrease your self doubt, not just with your spiritual development but also within other areas of your life. Embrace this journey as it arises from within and allow it to unfold naturally. As you do, you'll find that others will see this difference and your inner flame will shine more brightly, attracting to it those who will need your wisdom and guidance. But first how can this be so, if you don't first see it for yourself.

Trusting in myself and increasing my self belief has been the biggest challenge I have had to work through with my spiritual journey, especially as it pertains to my mediumship and my career. This has been a life long journey and will continue to be so as who I am is still a work in progress. This challenge has presented itself many times from the first time of walking on stage to demonstrate Mediumship, to speaking truth to a student who chose not to hear and to confronting the inadequacies of my marriage. All of which have an underlying contribution from me of not believing in some vestige of who I am. It is in these moments however, that my truth has been revealed as I look in the mirror and can therefore be empowered by shining a light on that dark corner and changing some small aspect of who I am or how I see myself. This has helped me immensely to find a greater peace within myself which these days, is plainly there for others to see. As a teacher I know that one of the greatest gifts I can give one of my students is to help them see themselves in this light too.

Something that goes hand in hand with Trust, is Fear. We don't trust, due to being fearful. Yet, fear is something that each and every one of us encounters in differing ways and to varying degrees. It can and will at different times affect your spiritual development, it can stifle the flow of personal growth or even hinder you getting your life to go in the directions you want it to. While there is no quick fix, I suggest working towards to minimising this in as many ways as you can. Start with the small things if you need to. Perhaps even unlocking your spiritual abilities is doing just that. Slowly but surely, if you become comfortable with the idea of stepping out of your comfort zone you'll find yourself in a place where you'll feel safe and confident, not worried about what others may think.

Fear is an everyday emotion. It drives us to do things which we would not normally do. It has us acting and behaving in ways that are not who we truly are: divine beings of love, created in the likeness of God. Each day, we are inspired by the energy of love to be who we truly are. Yet we react with fear and ultimately let ourselves down by not believing in ourselves, lacking the faith that we are beautiful beings in our own right, worthy of giving and receiving as we so deserve.

When was the last time you truly acknowledged this to yourself? When was the last time you gave for the sake of giving, expecting nothing in return but rejoicing in the feeling and emotion of giving to another in such a way? When was the last time you gave that very same gift to yourself?

Self-love is the enemy of fear. Feel fear and do it anyway because you love yourself enough to overcome life's hurdles that are placed before you. Feel fear and do it anyway because you love yourself enough to say to another. *"I'm sorry, but right now you have hurt my feelings and the disrespect I feel is unacceptable to me. I need your understanding right now."* Feel fear and do it anyway because you love yourself enough to accept that the Universe is how it is right now. You may not fully understand it all but trust and know, that because you are created in the likeness of God, all will be right in time.

One of the hardest things for any self aware traveller to do is to identify when one is operating and living with fear, especially when it is influencing our choices and actions.

Some tell tale signs to look out for are:
- An increase of negative and self-doubting thought forms

- A knot sitting in your stomach which isn't going away
- An inability to see things clearly
- Masking your true emotions
- Procrastination
- Dreams which contain symbols of fear – being chased, falling, attacked
- Any dream where you experience the emotion of fear in the dream
- An inability to make a decision moving you forward
- Overall loss of direction
- Frustration

Over the years I have come to understand that each time I reached a part of my journey where it was time to receive a new insight about myself and let it go, there was always fear precipitating the gaining of that understanding. This reflected directly in my work as a medium. Each time I released and overcame such an obstacle, my mediumship was vastly improved the very next time I made a connection with a loved one in the spirit world. By letting go of any negativity completely and replacing it with love, my energy and its makeup also experienced that change. As my aura is heavily involved in the communication process with Spirit, this change allowed a more seamless energy exchange between myself and Spirit, which therefore resulted in much clearer and better quality information coming through, including improved accuracy and the ability to receive more. Less negativity and blockages in my own energy meant Spirit having a clearer channel to communicate through. This to me has been proven time and time again, not just personally but also with many of ACOM's developing mediums.

We are able to apply this theory in every walk of life not just in mediumship. Experiencing the same changes of new understandings and letting go of blockages and fears will lead you to assimilate energetically more seamlessly into the Universe and its power of creation. This would allow you to bring forth your dreams and aspirations as you work towards manifesting your goals. Do not underestimate the power of energy and self awareness, as you become more aware and uncover what it is that holds you back.

So let's take some time to explore whether fear is walking with you as you turn your attention to opening up to Spirit. In your journal, I'd like you to answer honestly or as best you can the following questions. There is no right or wrong answers here, they are designed to help you shine a light and see where you could be holding yourself back.

1. *Please describe what your life will look like once you achieve being able to communicate with Spirit in the way you want to.*

2. *Acknowledge and write down any doubt that surfaced.*

3. *What three actions do you need to take now to work towards this picture.*

4. *In regards to your mediumship, what would you try now if you knew you could not fail?*

5. *What is stopping you from trying this now?*

Now we know what to look out for and how important overcoming fear is. What are some simple everyday actions we can do to move away and let go of our fears?

1. Breathe

Yes, I do mean that you become more aware of taking much deeper breaths and really filling your lungs. Be sure to appreciate and enjoy the gifts that sustain life. I also want you to think about it on a much larger scale and ask yourself the question *"Am I really "Breathing Life"? Am I taking it all in?"*

Take time to come back to what lifts your Spirit and makes you feel good. Is it such activities as going to the gym, walking the dogs, being with friends, taking a bath, enjoying a rock concert? Take some time to just enjoy!

2.   Acknowledge the Fear

This is the big one. Acknowledge that you are aware that you are currently walking with fear. Seek an understanding of why and where this applies in your life. Sometimes this is just as simple as being open enough to ask the question and accept whatever you feel the answer to be.

3.   Take Action

Once you uncover the answers above, then it becomes necessary to take action. There is no overcoming fear without this. Failure to do so will result in stagnation which can last years, even a lifetime if we allow it. When it comes to taking action, it's ok to take small steps in your own time, just as long as you are moving forward. For example, should you be unhappy in your work but not quite ready to make a big move, then start with researching the job advertisements. It is a step which can lead to another. I find at this point it helps me to play the 'worst case scenario' game. I ask myself *"If I was to do this, what would the worst outcome possibly be and if I didn't do this, what would the worst outcome possibly be."* I find that it helps me to clarify my thoughts and fears once I realise that the worst case scenario is usually something I can quite easily deal with.

There is one other simple, yet fun technique which I'd like to share with you. This technique I learnt from Peggy McColl, a New York Times bestseller, goal achieving expert and author of *Your Destiny Switch*. I think it is a too invaluable a tool not to pass on to you.

- Take a balloon and as you blow it up, be conscious that you are

blowing all your fear and negativity into that balloon. Once you have blown it up enough, don't tie it, but let it go so it flies around the room making that silly noise. Laugh and enjoy as you let it all go.
- Notice how much lighter do you feel.

Fear holds us back in so many ways. It is our choice however as to how much we allow it to control who we are and the lives we live. Breaking down a little fear each day is progress and goes hand in hand with allowing more love in your life. May you find, acknowledge and love the ugly duckling within as you release any fear keeping you from being the beautiful swan.

Patience; something we all need more of and when it comes to developing your spiritual abilities, the phrase 'patience is a virtue' could not be more applicable. Be aware that this is something that takes time and commitment. Like I mentioned earlier, a musician spends many hours in rehearsal and so too does an athlete spend many hours training for their particular sport. Attuning to your psychic senses is no different. You are retraining yourself, including your brain to communicate in new ways. Liken it to someone who through an accident may need to learn to talk or walk again. It takes time as the brain adjusts to new functionality.

Psychic development is also something that is best unfolded slowly so that the foundations are strong and sturdy. A lot of responsibility comes with using your spiritual abilities. Therefore a strong basis of spiritual understanding gained through growth and experience should be developed, along with the abilities so that you and your abilities continually inspire others positively.

Take every opportunity to practice using your new found abilities as much as you can. While working through this book, it is a good idea to set aside some time each week for meditation and to work through the exercises. Try using the same day and time each week, so that a routine and disciplined approach is established as part of your foundations. If possible, I would also suggest aligning your time with the time that one of our classes at ACOM is being run. Our class energies are able to assist you and your development in this way, just as if you were sitting in one of the circles. Most people do find it easier to meditate in a group rather than on their own. This is due to the cumulative energies all working as one. You can be a part of this too.

Lastly, practice as much as you can. Practice makes perfect certainly applies with psychic development, so take up every opportunity that is offered. And if like me, you don't have the patience to wait for an opportunity to come your way, create your own. I started with practicing psychometry, the art of reading someone's jewellery and writing down for them what I would receive. Then when I was ready, I would do the psychometry, face to face. You will find most of your friends quite happy to receive free readings, though I do suggest advising them that it is for practicing. This way you are relieved of any expectation on their part. It would not be fair of them to expect the same result of you at this point as they would from a professional. Keep in mind the saying *"Use it or lose it!"*

Before we move on, I'd like to urge you to take some time to think about why you have chosen to develop your spiritual abilities. Please write this down in your journal, so you can check in every once in a while to see if your reasons have changed. For me, I needed to understand life and its meaning on a deeper level and being able to live with a higher purpose. I found that unfolding my spiritual abilities helped me to do that. Helping others came second to that and I find that this is still true for me today.

Spiritual development is like most things, what you get out of it depends largely on how much you put into it. From the many people I have come across in regards to psychic development, those that sought to apply the learning and understandings on a day to day basis in all aspects of their live benefited the greatest in their psychic and spiritual abilities.

In this chapter:
- You will find that you have a natural strength with at least one or two abilities. Over time, aim to strengthen your weaker abilities so that all three are equally functional, creating a well rounded medium foundation.
- Journaling is an important technique that helps you to track and measure your individual progress throughout your development over weeks, months and even years.
- Fear presents itself in many ways. Can you identify how you feel fear and be aware of its effects on you? Once fear is addressed, improvement in your connection to spirit advances.
- Set aside time each week for meditation and development exercises, using the same day and time if possible to help establish routine and disciplined approach as part of your foundations. Practice as much as you can and create your own opportunities.

Their World is our World

> *In you, I see myself.*
> ~**Kerrie Wearing**.

Reflected through your own thoughts and beliefs the Spirit world is created in your own likeness of who you are. Your awareness of it is only limited by your thoughts and your ability to step outside of yourself and your humanness.

Try for one moment to see yourself not just as who you are right now in this incarnation, but also who you are as a soul. See yourself as the energy that has existed for eons of time, travelling many journeys and experiencing many lifetimes. See yourself as that part of yourself that knows so much more than just your everyday life. This part of who you are is just one aspect, one lifetime, one experience of your soul's energy. And it is this energy of the soul that is who you truly are.

With this understanding we can now work towards understanding gaining a bigger picture of the world that this part of ourselves resides in. Yes, we do have a part of our energy that resides in the spirit world. It is through this energy that we are all physically connected as one divine energy, with each and every one of us being part of God's creation. This aspect of our divine connection is experienced as that part of ourselves we recognise as our higher self. It is through this aspect of our humanness that we can bring forth and manifest the wisdom, knowledge and understanding of the spirit world as it pertains to Love.

Love is all there is in the world of spirit, so anything that falls outside of this is generated through the ego mind and calling forth your inner wisdom and power is the first step needed to raise your awareness of the Spirit world. It requires you to step outside of your humanness and ego to perceive beyond the realms of what you currently think is possible. The world of energy is all around you, connecting this world to the worlds beyond. I call it the world of energy for it is a more appropriate term for me, than our traditional understanding of the Spirit world.

You see, the Spirit world is actually a manifestation of the world of energy based on our thoughts and beliefs. Why is it that some people experience it so vastly different to another, or that some never experience it at all. When we die we experience a floating sensation much like lying on a water bed. This insight is being shared with me as I write from my brother Allen. He says *"Our thoughts and our feelings are maintained and*

co-exist as one. Not separate from one another as they do in human form. It is this very form of communication that a medium is working towards achieving with their spiritual abilities. Hence why understanding your intuition is important."

He goes on to say *"That once you are stabilised in your new world, there is a feeling of coming home and you do experience a life review. Not only are you shown how this current incarnation impacted you and others, but also how all of your other incarnations are connected here and what role they may have played in determining your life. There is no judgement, it is what it is and we go on from here. It is here then, that we become more greatly aware of all that truly entails who you are and we slowly start to disconnect from the human experience, allowing our energy to dissipate out into the collective world of energy. This process in your time is occurring gradually with the rituals of funerals and grieving all having an impact. The more grief the family left behind experiences the harder it is for us to let go. The bonds of love are forever strong, as is the purpose of our journey in coming together to experience life. These are never forgotten and the reason why mediumship works so well."* Allen then steps aside and introduces a young female energy who would like to share her story.

Julie's Story

"My experience is much the same, except I left behind more of a mess. I needed great fortitude to follow the original plan, as the pain I saw and felt from my family was often hard to bare. Many times I wanted to come back and assist them through whatever means I could, reincarnating or being around them in the presence of spirit. However I was always guided and reminded of the purpose behind my life ending in the way it did. I was left behind for others to find, strangled and violated it was not pretty however their love for me and one another shone through like never before. I did appear in dreams for them, especially mum trying to let them know that I was ok. I could see their pain. This was in December of 1993 and as the years passed, so too has their need for answers. It is here that the true purpose lies in understanding that we are all one, that we still exist no matter what and living in love."

At this point, I'd like to share with you some of my experience while I have been writing this chapter. It coincides with my auditioning for an Australian psychic television show which is a competition where the participants must complete a series of psychic challenges to reveal who the best psychic is. For me a show such as this is something I've always been in two minds about. While it serves a great purpose in bringing some understanding more into the mainstream awareness, the question is whether it is aligned with my purpose and the healing focus I approach my work with. While I am absolutely sure that auditioning and opening that door was the right path to tread, I only need to trust in my brother for him to clarify things for me in the most unexpected of ways. I was to meet the network people in a hotel in the city which was on Murray Street, my maiden name. To get to Murray Street, I needed to drive onto Allen Street. Which for me, as you can imagine was a major sign from my brother being that his full name is Allen Murray. While driving into the city, which from my home takes about an hour, I was constantly hearing the name Julie going around in my head and I was shown clairvoyantly that I would not end up being on this show, my path was to run along parallel to that of the show. During the first part of the audition which involved conducting a reading, I'm almost embarrassed to admit, that it didn't go so well to begin with. The information I connected with did not fit with the person I was reading at all. The network was very understanding and allowed me to try again, which worked fine. However, I knew something wasn't quite right though I wouldn't fully understand why until much later.

That night as I was going to sleep, my brother made himself known and explained that I would be involved with a TV show, just not this one, as the two purposes differ and the show for me was more in line with my work. When I questioned and doubted what he was saying, his response provoked lots of emotion and grief. He told me that our work together was the purpose behind him giving up his life. I always knew that without experiencing my grief and his loss through suicide I would not be who I am today and therefore not helping people the way I am. However, while I had considered this may have been Spirit's plan, it was not a belief I owned, until he said so. For me this beggared belief a little, as I wrestled with the feelings and emotions it brought up. Feeling the loss of my little brother again, I gained insight into the fact that he had been psychic himself, and not knowing how to deal with this it lead to a mental imbalance and not being able to fit into this world. All of which resulted in treating it with drugs and alcohol. In this, I understood his need to help others especially children and those who suicide. I also understood more that I am just the voice, part of a team and not always in the driving seat. I felt an even greater responsibility to do more and honour Allen's life. For no matter what I might fear or experience, it all pales in significance to the sacrifice he made.

From all of this we can glean that the Spirit world exists beyond normal boundaries and that we need to step outside of this to comprehend some of its working and composition. I say some, because I do not profess to know all of it, nor do I believe any one currently living can. It is not until we experience our own transition from this world can we truly understand the intricate nature of being alive in Spirit.

I do like to always approach my beliefs with realism and my understanding of the Spirit world is no different. So firstly, please cast your mind back to the chapter on understanding energy and how I described that energy as science currently knows it, being comprised of living vibrating atoms which hold information. It vibrates at varying degrees when it comes to our Spirit that is defined by one of two factors. The existence of LOVE or not. A lack of love, depicts a lower vibration as the energy becomes dull and lifeless. We know how this can be in our own lives, when we feel down, unhappy, depressed or negative compared to when we are happy and uplifted, we know we feel much lighter in our Spirit. So, filled with love the energy is vibrant, fast, congeals and blends easily, is on purpose and knows its true self.

Like all things, vibrating atoms of energy operate under the universal law of attraction and will collectively gather based on like attracts like and a synergy. This can give off the illusion that the Spirit world is comprised of varying levels. However, it is more appropriate to distinguish that these differences are created by awareness, understanding and the amount of love the energy and consciousness holds.

In defining the frequencies of the Spirit world as they pertain to mediumship specifically, let's begin with what is commonly known as the lower astral plane. This is the energetic frequency which lacks a lot of love and therefore we find energy and beings which exhibit fear, negativity, emotional pain, untruth and mischief. In our world an equivalent environment would be a gaol. In my experience though, I have seen many times the illusion of the lower astral plane only to find that the energies I encounter here need help to find the love that exists within themselves. To me, this is really no different to a lot of people in this world.

Secondly, our loved ones co-exist in a band of frequency that finds love operating on an everyday level. Their love for you still binds this aspect of their soul to you and it is this connection between your energy and theirs which leads to the experience of them still being around you, knowing you and your ongoing life as they do.

Then stepping beyond this frequency leads us to the vibration of love that operates purely on a spiritual soul level. For an energy with this much love vibration knows its true self as part of the Divine and is on purpose always. This is where you'll connect with a range of vibrational frequencies we associate with the energies of Angels, Spirit Guides, Ascended Masters, Goddesses and so forth. It is however also the frequency at which you'll experience your higher self. It is your higher self that links to this frequency of energy, to communicate with the energies at this level, assisting you to transcend the energy, experiences and information into your human consciousness. Therefore, higher self must be able to resonate at this vibration, for without this higher self link confusion would reign. It is our higher self which helps us to put it all into our everyday human context.

Beyond these frequencies there are many more, but for the

purpose of mediumship these currently do not come into play. This will however change in the not too distant future as the collective consciousness of the world opens itself up to the possibilities of life beyond what we currently know.

In this chapter:
- Part of our energy resides in the spirit world, this energy being our highest self.
- The spirit world is a manifestation of the world of energy that is based on our thoughts and beliefs.
- We are part of a team with Spirit, and not always in the driving seat!
- The Spirit world is defined by the vibration of love, or lack there of which identifies the lower astral plane. Our loved ones co-exist in the frequency of love. Frequencies of energies such as Angels, Spirit Guides, Ascended Masters, and Goddesses exist at the vibration of love that is on a spiritual soul level, the same level as your higher self.

Understanding your Spiritual Abilities, the 3C's and more

> *To see clairvoyantly, is to see with your heart.*
> ~**Anonymous Spirit Guide.**

When developing your spiritual abilities, it is important to remember that you are developing from a basis of skills and abilities that already exist within you. Your spiritual abilities will develop as an extension of the senses and abilities you already use in your day to day life. Your clairvoyance will develop as an extension of your sense of sight. Your clairaudience will develop beyond your current ability to hear and your clairsentience, is I'm sure a large part of your emotional self already. Failing to recognise this can set you back as coming to this learning with an acceptance of already what is, will help immensely.

As I mentioned previously, it is important to remember that you have strengths and weaknesses in these areas, and therefore you will find that you will have strengths and weaknesses with your gifts, just as you do with your everyday senses. Some people learn better or can grasp and express things better if they can see things or have a picture to work with, others are quite touchy-feely people and have no problem in expressing how they feel at all, while others struggle with that very much. This all affects our spiritual abilities, how we develop them and which of the gifts will be our strength or weakness. For those of you who may be physically impaired in either of these areas, then you are in for a treat because even though you may lack physically in one area this is in no way limiting as you find your other senses of psychic sensitivity heightened and being strengths for you.

For me, my clairvoyance coupled with my knowing and intuition were my strong points for a long time. I would receive a picture or symbol in my mind's eye and then receive an understanding of what this meant. Over time, through further development my clairaudience and my clairsentience have become part of my mediumship. I now have a more well rounded approached, however during development I have gone through times with each of them being a weakness or a strength.

As each individual is different in a variety of ways, from learning to perception, your abilities and development will be different also. Therefore, I can't stress enough how important it is not to get caught up in comparing your development with that of others. Developing your spiritual gifts is a unique experience, and you will only affect your confidence in doing this.

The 3 'C's explained

Clairvoyance

Clairvoyance, as with all the gifts, is a true visionary art form of communication. Your clairvoyance is perceived through channels of the mind, directly linked to the visionary tract. It's being able to see above the scope of what is being presented before the eyes. It uses your inner vision or third eye to process what is being communicated in the form of a picture in the mind's eye. Beyond this, opening your heart, you will learn to open your eyes to see things differently, to find things that didn't exist previously, now do. Therefore, opening your heart is directly related to widening your scope of vision and perception.

Without even realising it, we all have aspects of clairvoyance which we use on a daily basis. Our dreams, daydreams and imaginations are inner visions which all fall under the umbrella of the gift of clairvoyance. These we all encounter every day but mostly think nothing of them. Your psychic clairvoyant ability works not too differently to these inner visions, only the pictures are being received as a communication from an outside energy source, such as a spirit or another person's energy field, as opposed to receiving or creating the visions ourselves through your imagination or subconscious self. Let's do an exercise which will help you to understand this concept further.

Clairvoyance Exercise 1

1. Meditate and come to a place of peace within.
2. Close your eyes and imagine your bedroom.
3. See all of it, from the bed and its coverings right down to the items you may have sitting on your nightstand or bed side table.
4. Once you have a complete picture, open your eyes and write it all down in detail. This is your imagination.
5. Now we'll do the same exercise but for a friend. This should be someone whose bedroom you don't know so well, although you know they wouldn't mind you doing this. It may be a little easier for you, if they are sitting in front of you.
6. Close your eyes again, only this time in your mind ask to see their bedroom. Start with the detail of the bed or perhaps the colour of the walls. Ask to be shown what is on the bedside table. Once you feel you have all you can receive, open your eyes and write it

down in details.

7. Discuss the detail with your friend for validation.

8. Use your favourite process for grounding to close this exercise.

While I have chosen to use a bedroom for this exercise, as bedrooms are where we are most comfortable, it will work with any room you may choose. You may find that Step 2, seeing your friend's room is harder to do than seeing your own room in Step 1. This is expected, as you are seeing your friend's room using your clairvoyance, not your imagination. Try not to be too hard on yourself by expecting to get a full picture or every detail correct. Having just one item correct at this stage is a great success, and only your friend will know how meaningful that one item may be.

Dreams and their significance

I do see our dreams as being an aspect of our clairvoyance which is why I've included dreams in this section, and yet I do think they are an extremely under utilised area for receiving guidance and inspiration. Understanding our dreams is not as difficult as people might think and it only takes a little bit of work and attention to yield some great results.

Over the years I have had many dreams manifest in real life as Spirit use my dream state to communicate information I normally would not listen to or receive easily. One of the standout instances occurred in 2007 though the dream did not make complete sense until early in 2008.

I was at a psychic fair but on an upstairs level. Down on the next level I spied an old friend who was wearing some glamourous satin clothing, though with the shirt hanging out and looking a little untidy. This friend was with other people I knew and went behind some black curtains on a stage. As I was wandering around, a psychic stopped me and said I have a message for you. She told me that I was still healing. On waking from that dream, I knew something important was happening for my old friend, though perhaps it may not turn out as well as expected hence the untidiness of their appearance.

About nine months later I went to the taping of TV show which ended up baring remarkable resemblance to my dream. The black curtains fitted, the people in dream were all there on the day including my old friend. As we watched the taping, at one point a ring fell at my feet from the lady behind me, which I just picked up and gave back to her. Once the taping breaked and we could talk, this lady tapped me on the shoulder and said *"I want to tell you about my ring because it didn't just fall off, I wasn't playing with it. It literally jumped off my finger and landed at your feet."* She said the name of the crystal contained in it, but I can't really recall that. However, she said its meaning was *"It heals the healer."* So here was my message, just like in the dream. Fascinating!

Throughout history people have always sought to understand how dreams work and to gain insight from interpreting their dreams. Wikipedia states *"that Dreams have been described physiologically as a response to neural processes during sleep, psychologically as reflections of the subconscious, and spiritually as messages from gods, the deceased, predictions of the future or from the Soul, for symbology is the language of the Soul."* All of these encompass our understandings of dreaming up to this point in history. Certainly they are the unconscious state expressing itself, leaving you with insight into this aspect of yourself. Which for some can be a greater or truer part of who we are compared to the side of ourselves we present to the world.

In reality we all have a part of ourselves which we repress. Leaving no stone unturned when it comes to knowing one's self is a measure of someone with great spiritual insight and understanding. Therefore your dreams are a tool with great potential we should invest time and study to gain a greater understanding of who we are as our authentic selves.

Start with the knowingness that dreams exist for all. Whether you remember your dreams or not is not important at this point. Knowing you do dream is though. The more pertinent question is how do you

Understanding your Spiritual Abilities

tap into them and what do you do to understand the symbolism behind the dream language.

The dream state is most definitely a form of clairvoyance and a conservative starting point for those interested in developing psychic awareness. While there is plenty of information available regarding dreams from a physiological and psychological view point, I'll leave that to the expert psychologists and focus on how dreams relate to your spiritual and psychic development.

Let's begin by setting an intention to understand your dream state and commit to recording your dream insights in a journal each day. Record any imagery and most importantly any feelings associated with your dreams. If you don't remember the dream spend a few minutes thinking about knowing that you did dream and surmising how this may of felt. Write this down. A deeper part of you knows the information you are seeking which by consciously asking for it in a co-operative way will see this information filter through to your conscious state in time. Even if you only recall snippets of information which are not making a whole lot of sense to you, write these down. There is no right or wrong here and with more attention your recollections will improve.

Being the complex creatures we humans are, dreams allow us to process who we are and all that we take on emotionally and spiritually on many levels. From our subconscious to our intuition they provide a filter process for all of our surface level worries and our thoughts, helping us to work out what we need to let go off. Creatively they allow the expression of our spiritual self, giving us an avenue to open the doorway to Spirit.

To get more out of your dreams, it is important to understand at least a little of the different types of dreams we encounter.

Daydreams

While we tend to not give a lot of weight to daydreams, sadly this is a huge oversight on our part. Valuable information can be gained here as we understand that our day dreams can be clairvoyant information coming in, or insight into our daily occurrences. Begin to write these in your journal and treat them no different to your night time dreams.

Lucid Dreams

A lucid dream is when you actually realise you are dreaming while you are in the dream. A very powerful occurrence, as the potential for greater understanding is with you right in the moment, as both your subconscious and conscious states work together.

Learning to lucid dream allows:
- Learning to control and guide the outcome of your dreams which can assist you when overcoming fears and challenges you may be dealing with. For example, imagine dreaming you are speaking in front of a crowd and you know this would be uncomfortable for you, or a monster who may be getting the better of you. With lucid dreaming you can change the dream outcomes so you come out the winner and tap into your self empowerment.
- Interpreting the dream as it is happening, and asking the questions you need to know and being able to access the answers more readily.
- I often find myself doing this, as my higher self seeks to pass information through my daily crowded mind.
- Your mind cannot tell the difference between a dream, imagination or reality. So training yourself to dream the things you want to achieve, can help to manifest that reality in your life. Dreaming of writing your book, practicing your golf or living in that fabulous house you want helps you to generate how living that life would feel. An important aspect to hold onto when manifesting and co-creating your reality.

Nightmares

Are very important dreams to pay attention to. These dreams inform us of where we are suppressing a fear, problem or situation which is troubling us on a deeper level. By acknowledging this and bringing it into our awakened state we can begin to move towards healing, understanding and eventually letting go of whatever it is that is burdening us.

Recurring Dreams

Essentially this means that we lack the knowledge and insight from whatever the situation or dream can tell us about ourselves. Whatever it is your dream is trying to tell you, a recurring dream means we need to listen. Its frequency would indicate how important this insight is to you. So if you have a recurring dream start your dream study with this one, especially if it is quite frequent.

Processing Dreams

Some dreams serve the purpose of assisting to process your emotional and spiritual self, especially if these areas are largely suppressed within your waking consciousness. These dreams are often identified as busy, a replay of recent events and/or have a lot of emotion attached to them.

Prophetic Dreams

Most commonly dreams foretelling of future events. How do we know they are prophetic as opposed to symbolic? This will be covered a little later in the chapter.

Spirit Visitation Dreams

Yes, it is extremely common for people to experience visitations from their loved ones in Spirit. A visit such as this is often intended to reassure you and they occur most frequently just after your loved one has passed away, leaving you with a goodbye and a reassurance that all is ok. Sharing the joy of this message with others is the job assigned to the recipient of this dream as they have chosen you knowing they can get their message through loud and clear.

Over time such visitations are designed to show their continued support and love for you from where they are. So if you encounter a visitation at different times in your life, be sure to ask yourself *"Where in my life would I need support and guidance from my Spirit family"* and remember visits can be from the most unexpected members of Spirit. A true visitation dream is identified when your loved one's visit leaves with you an overwhelming feeling of love and peace. They feel quite distinct from the type of dream that may be associated with processing your grief.

Now that you are gathering some information in your journal and paying more attention to your dreams, let's begin the work to get more understanding out of your dreams. Take your dream journal and review the dreams, looking for repeating patterns and themes. Are there any common symbols used? Do you dream at a particular time each month, for example around the full moon? Patterns can help you identify emotional patterns in your life and what can be triggering them, while heightened dreaming around the full moon can be used to a greater potential by using that time for dream requests.

Request a Dream
1. Establish a sign that is to appear in your dreams to indicate each of the following dream types: a different signal should be used for each.
    - I am dreaming – great for lucid dreaming, for example a TV
    - My Answer Dream – for example, a smiley face
    - Spirit Visit – for example a pink rose

- Prophetic Dream – for example a Crystal Ball
2. Use your journal to write your dream request. A dream request may be for an answer to a specific problem or situation. It could be for a special loved one in Spirit to visit or even for you to get to know a Spirit Guide. There are no real limitations here.
3. Review your dream request every night before sleeping. Even place your dream request under your pillow if you feel that helps.
4. Write, draw or record your dreams daily.
5. Allow up to two weeks for your dream to appear, although I'm sure about a week may suffice. If you feel at the end of two weeks you have not received an answer, then ask for a sign to confirm whether you have or not. For example, ask to dream about one of your dream signals. This signal will provide your confirmation. Then look for the same signal throughout your dreams in the last two weeks.

When it comes to interpreting your dream language, the language of the soul, please refer to the section on Symbolism and Meaning in Chapter 9. As I've described there, I believe that the symbolism we receive for all inspired communication, such as dreams, meditations and spirit communication can all be interpreted the same way. After all, its our own mind, body and soul receiving the information and trying to understand it. Why would we receive information we cannot possible make sense of right now. I don't think we would.

Clairvoyance is an important ability as it helps to bridge the communication gap between cultures and languages. To tell a medium "*I was a nurse*" is easier to do with a picture and can be done no matter the ethnicity of the spirit the medium is communicating with. This way the blending of all walks of life can occur. There are however, some points to make in regards to the pictures we receive. One symbolic picture I work with is the yellow daffodil. In Australia this is a fundraising symbol for cancer so whenever I see it, to me that is what it means. Occasionally, though it can mean something other than that to the people I am reading for. I recall one family whose mother was Welsh and they told me later that the yellow daffodil is the Welsh flower symbol for women and that they had a photo of their mother with daffodils all around her. This is what my bringing through the yellow daffodil meant for them. So there are instances when the meaning for our symbolic pictures can step outside of our framework of knowledge, as I would never have known this Welsh reference.

Similarly, when we work with pictures it opens our minds to unfolding stories as the pictures move across our third eye like a movie. When this happens do not question it and try to talk it through as it is happening for you. It is the act of acknowledgement and speaking this truth that allows for the flow of communication to continue. Halt the flow with doubt or trying to make sense of it all and you will very quickly find the images stop.

Lastly, it is important to note that there are two forms of clairvoyance. Subjective clairvoyance is where the images form within your mind space and predominately in the area of the brow or third eye energy center. This is probably the most common form and is certainly how I mostly experience my clairvoyance. While detail levels vary for everyone, try not to get caught up in how much detail and just work with what you do receive. The second form of clairvoyance is known as objective clairvoyance as the images appear outside of yourself. For example, you may see images forming on a wall or in the energy of the person you are speaking with. While this is a rarer form of clairvoyance, to develop this ability further it is as simple as spending time doing an open eyed meditation and focusing on a candle while you meditate.

Clairvoyance Exercise 2

1. Take a moment to still yourself and find that space within you

Understanding your Spiritual Abilities

that speaks of peace, wisdom and truth.
2. Focus your mind's eye on an object in front of you and allow the imagery to unfold as the energy of the object speaks to you.
3. This exercise can be done with eyes open or closed, therefore helping to develop both forms of clairvoyance. Should you have an interest in crystal balls then this would be the exercise to help you develop scrying, the ancient technique of using an object, mainly crystal balls to predict the future.
4. As you become a little more comfortable introduce an object that belongs to someone you know, or if using a crystal ball have them sit with you. This way you begin working towards receiving real and relevant information for people.

At first the imagery may not be clear or in focus, and you may not understand what any of it means which is not really important right now. What is important is that you are opening up the channels involved and preparing them to receive information. Have fun with it and try not to be too hard on yourself.

Clairaudience

Clairaudience is the art of hearing with a sensitivity beyond that which we currently know. Imagine what it would be like if you thought you heard other people's thoughts. This is how subjective clairaudience works. A thought to thought transference, where you will receive names, dates, songs and even conversation snippets within your own mind.

This ability is a little trickier to develop as it is often harder to decipher another's thoughts from that of your own. However, once we become adept at hearing this way, the patterns and irregularities in another's thoughts become distinguishable within the mind without you even needing to worry. Much like the brain quickly learns to distinguish pain or hunger from satisfaction, so too does the brain learn to distinguish a clairaudient communication to that of your own thoughts. Our job then is to just learn to trust ourselves that when we think it might be someone else's thought, then it probably is.

It's worth mentioning here, that when we first start out wanting to develop this gift, it is very common for people to expect with clairaudience that we are going to hear spirit in the way we hear one another, outside of our head. This was true for me even. I had not come across anyone or any information while learning that clearly explained what to expect. It wasn't until many years into my psychic awareness that I had an "a-ha" moment about all the thoughts and channelled wisdoms I had been receiving from my guides being clairaudient experiences. It does take me some time to get it every now and then.

Hearing outside of our own bodies is known as objective clairaudience, and while this can and does happen, especially during those moments as we are slipping into sleep, it is quite rare for someone to have their clairaudience developed to this level. Many of us have the occasional experience where we hear our names being called, but in the fifteen years I have been meeting and teaching people about Spirit, I have only met one person with such ability. While we might think having such an amazing gift would be wonderful, I do believe it could present a whole gamut of other problems, leaving it very difficult to maintain a balance between living in this world, which is what we are here to do, and communicating with the spirit world as opposed to escaping to it.

Clairaudience Exercise 1
1. Keeping with the bedroom theme, although this time, instead of seeing your bedroom try to hear it. Listen for the regular sounds you encounter while you are in your bedroom. Do you normally hear the garbage collector from your bedroom? If so, then listen for this sound. Can you hear the birds chirping as you start to stir in the morning? It's a nice sound to wake up to. What else can you

Understanding your Spiritual Abilities

hear?

2. Once you have completed Step 1, I'd like you to 'hear' some different sounds in your mind, starting with your favourite song of the moment. Hear it in your mind; hear the music and the lyrics. It's ok to dance too if you like.

3. Try another sound now, like the starting and revving of a motorbike. And another, much softer now. I'd like you to listen for the 'meow' of a cat.

It's a good idea to write down your experience. You may even find your other spiritual abilities working as well. Did you see the motorbike or a cat for instance?

Clairaudience Exercise 2

Another simple exercise to develop your clairaudience is to concentrate and focus on your listening. How many times do we talk with people while our minds are actually thinking about other things? I know I'm a culprit for doing this. So bring the focus back to what is being spoken, really hear what people are saying to you. You may be surprised at the insights that can be gained.

Clairaudience Exercise 3

This exercise can be easily carried out almost anywhere you listen to music. While listening, try to distinguish between the layers of music. When the songs are compiled there are many tracks layered on top of one another, all coming together to produce the finished song and what it is we hear. Most people with little or no musical knowledge will only hear the complete and final product, while a drummer will hear the drum beats more distinguishably than a keyboardist or guitarist.

Try listening hard enough to identify which layers you can distinguish. You'll be surprised at what you'll find. I'm sure I've heard vocal tracks on a Gwen Stefani song that seem hidden on the surface.

As I explained earlier, our spiritual abilities are an extension of our human senses. With this in mind, you'll find that your clairaudient ability will respond by activating it with sounds from this world that specially work on the energy of the aura and our chakras. While this can be achieved with everyday music we love and we know it lifts our spirits, such music inspired therapy as Tibetan singing bowls, crystal bowl therapy, meditations conducted with chants or my particular favourite Native American Drumming will all help to openly activate the channels and neural pathways of the brain needed to make clear audient communications from Spirit. So again, relax and find some simple fun ways to enjoy these activities, and if you're like me and many others, you will be receiving words and thoughts in your mind not realising it's clairaudience because you will still be waiting to hear Spirit's voice next to your own.

Clairsentience

Clairsentience is the art of recognising and understanding emotion and physical sensations that are not your own. I like to differentiate clairsentience from that of your own inner knowing as I think this helps you to understand the differences and your abilities more intimately.

Clairsentience is an extremely common ability and of all the spiritual gifts it is most often the one which is hard to detect. If you have any clairsentient ability, you'll find it very common to encounter extreme mood swings, which can change at a moment's notice. One moment you can be peaceful and happy, going along swimmingly, only to have a drastic downturn in your mood for no apparent reason. I see this quite often in teenage girls. You will also find yourself easily overwhelmed and/or highly stimulated or drained when you visit such places as shopping centers and hospitals.

I remember when my mother was in hospital for a month prior to

Understanding your Spiritual Abilities

her heart bypass. I was visiting almost every day, taking in the necessities, when the first couple of visits left me feeling so drained that a sleep on the lounge was needed after to recover. Once I questioned this, I realised that my energies were giving out healing to others in the coronary ward leaving me with little left to get along. So, on the next visit, I prayed and asked that I kept what I needed, so that I had more energy and strength to cope with my own situation. From this visit on, my energy levels where fine. Being clairsentient, I guess you would also relate to having the common experience of attending a friend's BBQ, only to feel uncomfortable as you arrive and thinking to yourself that they've not long had an argument.

All this sensitivity can be attributed to your clairsentience. When developing psychically this ability can be extended upon to not only gain a broader picture of the emotions of others, but also to allow Spirit to relay messages regarding emotion and their physical experiences. For example, should one of your regular Spirit Helpers be a family member or friend who crossed over from a heart attack, you may feel them about by the presence of a subtle pain in your chest. Kidney pain if they suffered kidney disease or shortness of breath if they encountered breathing difficulties, like my brother with his asthma. Your Spirit Guides may also indicate their presence or confirm messages by way of sending tingles down your spine or a sense of warmth up your arm. These are just a small sample of the way clairsentience works.

Clairsentience Exercise 1

1. Again keeping with the theme of connecting with your bedroom, close your eyes and think of it. This time I want you to get a feel for it. How does it feel to you? Feeling the difference on your side of the bed to that of your partner's side? Is there a difference at all? Once you have uncovered some sense of the energy, open your eyes and write it all down in detail.

2. Once you have finished connecting with your own home, do the same exercise for your friend again. If you found doing this exercise a little difficult with your home, then try doing your friend's home first and then try again with your home after.
3. Discuss what you feel you have uncovered with your friend for validation and understanding.

Clairsentience Exercise 2

1. Try to obtain a photo of a friend or relative you don't know too well. This photo could be either of someone living or passed, however if they are living please seek their permission first as you are about to encroach on their privacy. Those in Spirit will offer their permission by working with you or not.
2. While holding the photograph, take a moment to centre yourself and find that space of peace. Meditate beforehand if that helps.
3. As you hold the photograph become aware of the feelings and sensations you experience. What kind of personality do you sense this person has? Are they happy or a little sad?
4. Imagine yourself in the photo with them as if you are talking with them, open your heart and let the energy of the connection speak to you.
5. Record your thoughts and speak with your friend in an effort to receive your validation.

You may like to try this using your children's bedroom. It may help you feel how restful or not their rooms really are. This is something my children understand and feel about their own rooms. They will let me know when the energy becomes a little unsettled and then we can go about rectifying this by either just through talking something through, rearranging the furniture, using a bit of basic Feng Shui or even using a few crystals. This all seems to help.

Knowing and Intuition – the God-Self Connection

As mentioned earlier, I feel it is important to differentiate between the 3'C's and your inner knowing or intuition. Your intuition is that part of you that ultimately knows all and will lovingly guide you towards a life of prosperity, harmlessness and the gifts of insight and understanding, especially towards others.

I'm sure many of you have had the experience of knowing something but would say you don't know how you knew it, you just know you do. Or you could have had something happen only to realise and say to yourself *"Yeah, I knew that."* Well, that's your inner knowing talking.

Opening up and strengthening your intuition, I believe, is not really something that can be taught with exercises like the ones described above. To me, there is really only one way to achieve this awareness to a point that your intuition is actively involved in how you guide your life. That is to trust in and to act on your intuition. By being a little brave and leading a life where you make your decisions, big or small, based on what feels right for you, as opposed to what you think you should do, will see a flourishing inner knowing develop.

I personally try to make all my decisions based on how I feel about the choices I have been presented with and whether or not they sit peacefully in my gut. This is certainly easier to do sometimes more than others, like when you are trying to decide which dress to buy or which party to go to at Christmas. Other times though it can be far more difficult.

For me one of those times involved my career and making the choice to focus full time on my mediumship. I was working full time as a purchasing officer, with my children in full time before and after school care and had recently started to focus more seriously on my mediumship. For the last few months I had been doing mediumship demonstrations in people's homes two to three times a week. They had been far more popular than I anticipated and while I had only been doing this for about three months, I was already being presented with having to make a decision as to whether to leave my job, which was not working for me any longer, or to keep growing the mediumship business, however that unfolded.

At the time it was quite gut wrenching because in my heart I knew what felt right but was still faced with concern for my family obligations, the mortgage and what my husband felt. Here I was giving up a steady reliable income to work with an uncertain income and asking my husband to trust in this. In the end, I'm grateful I had the courage and the support of my husband to make the right decision, as look to where it has lead. That whole experience certainly showed me that when you do follow what is in your heart, your expectations are often exceeded if you allow Spirit to work its magic. I never expected at that point in time to be where I am today, living a life, sharing in Spirit with others like you.

Here is one little, yet very powerful exercise, which can help you to identify and strengthen your intuition. I call it 'Your Intuitive Navigation System', and from my limited knowledge of Kinesiology, it uses similar principles and is based on using your body and the stomach muscles much like you would a pendulum.

Exercise for developing your intuition

1. Sit quietly for a moment, just so you are able to concentrate on the task at hand.
2. Focus your awareness to your stomach region. We are going to ask our stomach two questions, both times taking note of the reaction.
3. Ask yourself a question you know to be answered with a 'No', such as *"Is my name Allen?"* Please pay attention to how your stomach is feeling. The response will be different for everyone,

although it may be along the lines of something similar to your stomach tying itself in knots. Whether it is this or something else, this is how you now identify your 'No'. How your stomach reacts with your 'No' will not change, it will be the same, always.

4. Now ask yourself a question you know to be true and is answered with a 'Yes' such as *"Am I a girl?* or *"Am I a boy?"* Again, pay attention to how your stomach is feeling. This response should be quite different and in contrast to the previous 'No' answer.

5. This is now how you identify your 'Yes'. How your stomach reacts with your 'Yes' will not change, it will be the same, always.

6. Once you are comfortable with being able to tell the difference, you are ready to ask yourself a more significant question, and see what your very own intuition is telling you about it.

7. Let's try asking some questions about your Spirit Guide. It's best to start simply with Yes or No questions, such as, *"Are you male?"* Or *"Are you female?" "Do you have blonde hair?"* and *"Are you an Angel?"*

Remember, this little tool is extremely useful for all aspects of your life, when meeting new people, or when trying to make decisions regarding where to go and what to do in life. I suggest starting with the small issues and concerns first, then, as you gain confidence include the more important things as well.

It is important to use this exercise as often as possible at first. This will heighten your awareness of yourself, from your intuition to how you feel when responding to different energies, be those people, places or situations. Developing this unique little tool is also far more reliable than any crystal pendulum; there is nothing that can beat relying on your own intuition. You will find that over time the need to ask the questions will subside as you become more adept at listening to the immediate responses of your body and your intuition.

Psychics and Mediums both use the same spiritual abilities to receive information through the energy though there are two distinct different purposes. Psychic premonitions are about the occurrences which we map out in our lives through the process of creation. A psychic focused on this work will tune into the energies level associated with this and receive information via the appropriate channels using their psychic abilities. Predominately focused on life issues such as relationships, work, home, money and all that defines our human existence, psychics provide guidance and understanding to assist when we are presented with these challenges and difficulties.

A medium on the other hand has a different focus and therefore will tune into the energies levels associated with a greater perspective of the whole. Our level of awareness, beliefs; conscious and unconscious help to unlock this. While receiving information from here uses the same spiritual abilities that all psychics do, mediumship and communicating with the afterlife has its roots connected in a much deeper spiritual purpose. Proving life after death exists, awakens within us a light that speaks to our soul and ignites recognition of our true purpose. A purpose that identifies we are connected to the Divine and that at some point we will return home. Mediumship is the tool and doorway to help people understand that we are first and foremost spiritual beings living a human experience.

This does not mean that being a medium is better or more important than being a psychic. Each have their place and purpose, and I'm sure that there are some excellent psychics who make a difference for others every day. So just what is it that sets apart the difference in the psychic process to that of the mediumship process. As I said earlier, psychics and mediums do use the same abilities to receive the information, our clairvoyance, clairaudience and so forth. So can every psychic become a medium?

Absolutely, I believe so. We all have our own potential and purpose to reach, the change is brought about with a change in beliefs and awareness. There is no one specific thing that must change for this to happen as each individual is different, however a belief and willingness to change from where you are is all that is needed. For me personally, I spent seven years working as a psychic using aura readings as my tool of trade. It was in 2002 as I joined a new development group that the very first night during the meditation, Spirit told me I was there to raise my awareness. In my ignorance, I thought I was already a person with a heightened awareness, looking back now though I chuckle at how unaware I really was. The gift in that journey and those first seven years of psychic work however, has left me blessed to have the best of both worlds.

In this chapter:
- The three C's of mediumship are Clairvoyance being the ability to see, Clairaudience being the ability to hear and Clairsentience, the ability to feel.
- Dreams are a valuable tool to help develop your clairvoyance.
- Developing your own 'Intuitive Navigation System' is a simple and powerful way to strengthen and use your intuition.

Living with Spirit

> *Mediumship; known by many, practiced by some and lived by few.*
> **~White Feather.**

When we first begin to raise our spiritual awareness and understand there is more to this life than we first perceived, we begin to notice universal signs and an increased amount of seemingly co-incidental occurrences. Almost as if the universe is whispering to you.

In doing so, we slowly begin to think of ourselves as spiritual beings. In fact, there is a common expression used in the spiritual community *"We are spiritual beings having a physical experience."* While I believe this to be true, I also think the use of this expression is quite often bandied about with little thought for what the words truly mean or what living such a concept would be like.

If we are a spirit first and a human second, what do you think life would look like for you or for someone who truly lives from that perspective?

In my experience they are someone who easily understands that the way forward is always through love. While they may still encounter difficulties in life, their ability to approach these challenges seeking insight and understanding is first and foremost their priority, as not only do they know this is where all solutions lie, but they also inherently know that their souls only purpose is one of learning, evolution and enlightenment.

They would see through the illusion to the truth and the heart of matters, while easily seeing the essence of people. Seeing the light in all, even those clouded in darkness and not let judgement stand in their way.

They heed the call of their own heart knowing that to love thyself is a symbol of loving God and this great universe, for in so doing they are loving all of creation. While living this, they are mindful of giving to others but not to the point of self sacrifice as this hinders the ability to love freely.

Turning away from engaging in negativity and supplying any energy to such matters, becomes a natural instinct as they seek to maintain an energy of positivity, joy and upliftment. Knowing their own Spirit rejoices in this as well as being fully aware of the energetic contribution they make to those around them and the Universe as a whole.

Baring in mind the intricacies of this world, each and every one of us can express all of this quite differently, from simple smiles, loving gestures with a mindfulness and awareness as one goes about raising their children and providing for their family. To others who feel a greater call to share this knowledge and understanding with others, so they too can rejoice and walk with peace and understanding.

Life itself will flow more easily with this awareness of living from our Spirit. The universe leads us forward consciously through the flow of synchronicity, God's lighted pathway as I like to call it, which is more commonly recognised as those 'co-incidences' that cross our path. I prefer the term synchronicity as to me it feels that I am valuing this in my life more whereas using the term 'co-incidences' tends to devalue the true essence, giving the event or occurrence almost a flippant view of it. When really, nothing could be further from the truth.

Living from your Spirit will naturally bring about a sense of harmony resulting in a life of balance, spiritual maturity and a flow of regularly occurring synchronistic events designed to move you forward to achieving your true life's purpose. You won't even need to try. There is no hard work about making this happen, apart from living your true Spirit. While this at times may not always be easy for a variety of reasons, such as not living to other people's expectations of you, even if they most likely are family. Or often having the realisation that in this moment you are not truly happy, and that it is only you letting yourself down in some way. Someone living with Spirit knows that in facing life's challenges there is ALWAYS a higher purpose and we need only to look for it.

For a long time now, I have been at peace with my brother's suicide. Once I began opening up spiritually I was always of the understanding that without that experience and his loss, I wouldn't be who I am today. This is something I still feel today and while there was and still is some pain, he really gave me the greatest gift of all. Myself!

(Tears flowing just now... as I thank him yet again.)

Going forward over the next couple of days, I shall be mindful of watching for all the car registration plates which have the letter KEZ on them. This is one of his regular signs to me which symbolises he is around and that everything is ok. He called me "Kezza" and was the only one to do so and is now the only one allowed to.

In your life there will be many ways like this that Spirit will begin the first stages of communicating with you. This is not only to reassure us, but to also remind us that we are spiritual beings ourselves. Over the years I have heard many, many stories regarding signs and synchronicities which involve music, animals, birds, butterflies, feathers and much more. There was even one father a little more keen to get his message across than that.

This was a few years ago when I still did face to face readings at home. I was sitting with Angela and was making a connection to her father Ron. The names have been changed to protect their privacy. During this session, there were two magical moments that happened.

I said to Angela that Ron made himself known at home by the presence of physical activity such as lights flickering and doors opening. Well it was only a moment or two later that the door opened to the room we were in. I had never experienced this door opening of its own fruition before, so I understood this to be Ron's way to let his daughter Angela now that it truly was him, as what was to come next was extremely important.

Ron was quite an astute man and was quick to know and recognise my boundaries as a medium, thereby delivering the next message without me realising it. I continued, saying to Angela that her dad was quite proud to see that she was keeping her father's memory alive in her little boy. He showed me a picture of a little boy praying, indicating that he could see his grandson praying to him at night before bed. He went onto to say that as the little boy grows, her dad will forever be in this little boys heart. This was a nice sentiment I thought, but one which had so much more meaning to Angela. At the end of the session, Angela shared with me that her son needed a heart transplant and with Ron saying he would grow in her son's heart, she understood this to be her dad's way of telling her the new heart was coming, and he was right. I heard a few months later that the little boy did indeed receive his new heart and all was going well.

For me, as the medium I was so impressed with Ron's ability to get his message across, as at the time if I had of received that communication clearly and directly I would have struggled with delivering it. I would have worried about creating false hope and while I acknowledge that as my own doubt, the reality is that we psychics and mediums are never one hundred percent accurate either. This is the responsibility of the work of a psychic and a medium, which should never be forgotten. But more on that later.

Communicating with Spirit

There really is only one prerequisite for communicating with Spirit and that is having and living with an open heart. In all the years I have assisted people to make their own connections to Spirit, the only people I have seen struggle with this are those who find opening up to others difficult. Not trusting others or allowing others to get too close to us can hinder our learning to communicate with Spirit. If this is part of who you are you must first learn to break this down and overcome the issue of distrust which I know for someone who has been hurt numerous times and has established a wall of protection in this way, can find this challenge extremely daunting.

My higher self interjects again here...

"The heart lies in the chasm of our chest just as we live within the chasm of the universe. Reaching forth to experience Spirit is beyond controlled human awareness. Opening your heart and living from this space releases the bonds of the mind as we focus more on our feelings. It is here, through emotion, that the key to not just Spirit but the Universe lies."

Imagine being able to understand how each and every person feels without any words passing your lips. This is the quandary a medium faces on a day to day basis. It is often said that a medium feels with their heart but sees with their soul. This is true to some degree however it is more pertinent for a medium to see with heart and soul. Thoughts and feelings all as one, as my brother Allen described in a previous chapter.

When I first began my role as a teacher of mediumship, I was somewhat blind to the intricacies of mediumship. These were learnt along the way as I mustered the courage to continually look within my own soul. I very quickly moved from thoughts and word of *"What do I think about this?"* to *"How do I feel about this?"* These words are a staple of my vocabulary, inner dialogue and thought processes and I recommend they become part of yours to.

From here, you may question *"C'mon where are the techniques to teach communicating with Spirit?"* They will come, but first please allow me some rhetoric as I share with you a story. Over the years there has been many times when I have gotten in my own way. Fear, doubt, high expectation and control have all been part of me that I have worked at slowly, to relinquish control of how I think things are meant to be. Whether, it has been the outcome of a reading or in other areas of my life. Early on it was enough that I was learning all this about myself without the need to change it just yet. Then came a time when enough was enough and change needed to come. While having Spirit on my side, I was confronted with the very thing I feared the most, the loss of ACOM and my career. Had I known then what I know now, that facing a fear this significant frees you to allow the unexpected to flow more forcibly, leading you to places you can never imagine at the time, I would have accepted things a little easier, though perhaps not gained as much from the experience. Having the belief that the universe provides and everything happens for a reason is one thing, but living those beliefs is quite another.

When I needed to close the rooms I rented for ACOM while losing the majority of the student client base I had established, my first inclination was to run and return to mainstream work and say *"at least I tried."* This sense of doubt and indecision about my direction lasted a good couple of years and was often compounded by the financial struggle we faced at home. It really wasn't until beginning the writing of this book in its current form that my true sense of purpose has shone through. I am an educator of Spirit, not so much a messenger and while I have known this for a while, my sense of living it, valuing it and putting it out there for others to experience without doubt has been a long time coming.

So I say to you, first and foremost in your experience of communicating with Spirit, eradicate the doubt of who you are. Love and accept yourself for the light of love you are. Do not allow others and what they may think of you to deter you. Be strong and centered in this belief of yourself. Yes, Spirit will guide you to this knowing and a life that exudes this. However, I can tell you that the road is a much easier one if you understand this and you will be much better placed in life and your efforts to communicate mediumistically, if you start owning that sense of self NOW!

Exercise to communicate with Spirit

Communicating with Spirit is best done when allowing Spirit to do most of the work. However, there are a few things we need to do in readiness to receive the information.

1. Raise your vibration by way of meditation and prayer. Find some quiet time and meditate preparing your own consciousness to let go of its everyday focus. The meditation provided in the chapter *Your Spirit Team* would be a great help.
2. Welcome Spirit in to communicate with you through sending that very thought out into the world of Spirit and thank them for their willingness to do so. During this process visualise your own energy opening and energising, being ready to receive. I personally visualise this with each individual chakra so that I am working towards my own energy being as open and receptive as it can possibly be. Spirit can and will use any or all of our chakras to make a connection. The aim here is to work towards achieving

our own energy blending seamlessly with the energy of Spirit as we come together as one.

3. Honouring the wonder of it all. Here I generally honour my own contribution, including my abilities and understanding, while thanking those in Spirit who will work with you and for the opportunity to serve. Keeping a space of gratitude and service will work towards being mindful maintaining humbleness.

Invocation to Spirit (sample)

"Divine Spirit, I am here before you to serve and honour the presence of Spirit within this world. In service please use me as a channel for light, love and messages of validation in an effort to prove the continuous existence of the soul and offer the opportunity for others to heal. I call upon the light of love to flow through me as it flows through all people and all things. May it enhance the flow of communication, bridging the gap between your world and ours.

I welcome those in Spirit who wish to step forward and communicate with their friends and family. I thank them for the opportunity to speak on their behalf and know that together we work towards healing and greater understandings for all involved. I can only hope I do you justice.

I honour my own abilities and understandings. My clairvoyance, my clairaudience, my clairsentience and my knowing and intuition. It is with these abilities that I strive to be the best medium and teacher that I can be, while endeavouring always to deliver this work with love, understanding and humbleness. Staying true to all that I am. My love for this work knows no boundaries as I am honoured to be presented with this opportunity to serve and thank you for the ongoing support.

Thank you."

4. As you sit quietly and mentally voice all of this, become aware of how different the energy starts to feel around you. Lighter and like a warm fuzzy blanket, thick with love. This is the first indication that things are starting to happen.

5. Lastly, as Spirit steps forward to work with you, and they will because you have asked for them with respect. Know that your job is to just acknowledge out loud all that you receive.

I would suggest here that it would be a good idea to record this sitting, so you can work freely in the moment but have the information to work through and analyse later. Acknowledging all that you receive is not as difficult as you may think. If we break it down, just voice out loud whatever you feel, see in your mind's eye or think. So if you start to feel 'funny', 'sick' or get a pain somewhere specific, this is your clairsentience working and highly likely the pain in your chest could be the heart attack of the energy working with you. Same goes for the nausea associated with cancer or the loss of thought associated with dementia. Even your thoughts at this point are not just your own. So embrace it all by acknowledging them, this will keep the flow going.

Tip: *If your acknowledgement and understanding of the message is correct. i.e. you identified the male as a male, said the thoughts they have passed you and voiced out loud the correct ailment then when acknowledged correctly, this message will move on making way for the next message of communication. Simply put, let's say you were communicating with my brother Allen. It is common for him to step forward and pass you two pieces of information. A wheezing feeling in the middle of your chest, is his way of saying he had asthma. This is one way I know he is about. Or he may even provide a choking sensation around the throat associated with his passing. Sadly, he did pass by hanging himself, though he is very adept at passing this to students to assist in their development. If you identify the subtle feelings and messages you receive in this way, correctly, the feeling and message will immediately lighten and leave, making way for the next communication to come in. This happening in this way is your confirmation. If you've got it wrong, the message will either not leave or it will return again until such time as we do get it right. We are speaking on their behalf after all, so I'm sure they want to ensure its all passed on in the way they intend it as much as they can.*

Early on though, it is not so important as to whether the information you receive is correctly validated or not. That is a bonus right now, what is important is that you are opening the channels of communication. Mediumship is a bit like a dripping tap. One drop of water falling allows the next one to flow through, so to with mediumship. Voicing it and allowing it to flow will allow the next pieces of information to flow directly behind. So try not to catch yourself up at this point by trying to understand what it all means. That will come in time, it is far simpler than you think and it is then that you begin working towards the quality and accuracy of your information.

I use this exercise regularly with my teaching programs from beginners right through to the more experienced classes. It works effectively each and every time due to the support of those in Spirit who step forward to assist us. One of my favourite things to see in a workshop is people finally gaining the understanding of how simple it can be, all be it somewhat subtle and for a group reading coming together and being validated as a connection for someone in the group.

6. Once you start to feel the energy lighten and lift, like your blanket has been taken away. It is time to ground yourself and release the excess energy while offering a prayer of thanks and gratitude.

To ground, visualise a beautiful silver lotus blossom on the ground before you with its petals open and shinning brilliantly. Its petals slowly start to absorb all of your excess energy and you feel this as the energy slowly starts to drain away from the top of your head, draining down around your shoulders and torso. Your excess energy continuously pours forth into the lotus. Once the flower has its fill and you feel the energy finally drain away from the bottom of your feet, visualise the petals of your lotus flower closing in upon themselves. It is returning all this beautiful energy to the Universe to be used where it is needed most for healing.

For further grounding techniques please refer to the chapter on Raising your Vibration.

INTERPRETING THE MESSAGE: Symbolism and Meaning

In the moment when we receive a communication from Spirit, our own mind will kick in and try to understand what it all means. My advice here is to allow the process to unfold to a point that the communication holts for a time. This indicates that what your Spirit communicator is trying to say is complete and they are allowing us some time for recognition. Analysing prior to this will have you trying to interpret without all of the information and therefore most likely missing the point. Spirit always has the communication process in hand and we are best to try and trust in this.

In my experience the best way to release the communication is to acknowledge out loud by verbalising or writing it down. Many mediums approach this aspect of the work with the mantra *Give it as you get it:* This is true to some extent however, there are two considerations which need to be factored into this. Firstly, all of the communications you receive from the Spirit world, whether from loved ones, spirit guides, angels or any other energy, are being received through your frame of reference. This means your framework of beliefs and knowledge does influence the information you can receive in many ways. John Edward, the world famous medium is one example of this. If you have watched him work with some regularity, you will notice his ability to be very detailed and specific with health issues. His having worked in the medical arena has an influence with this, just in the same way that a medium who is Italian, Greek or Asian will relate more directly to a Spirit communicator of the same ethnicity, more than I am capable of. Understanding their culture and way of life allows the Spirit to elaborate and detail so much more of their own lives.

Secondly, I think we have a little more responsibility in doing the work than just delivering it as we get it. Mediumship is supposed to leave people with a sense of love and healing which is heavily influenced by how the medium delivers the information.

I recall starting with a new group a few years back which was at a new crystal shop, a little ways from where I live. I didn't know the owners of the shop, so was still in the process of getting to know them and they me. I am always very conscious of who I work with in any capacity, trying to ensure that we approach our work similarly which ensures a synergy in the energy and that our messages to the market is also in tune. As they were to also join the group this was going to take care of itself one way or another, were my thoughts.

I usually start the group off using their abilities and delivering information very early on and this class was no different. One young lady volunteered to be blindfolded and was instructed to just say out loud whatever it was that she saw, heard or felt. The blindfolding helps to minimise distractions, allowing focus and stopping people worrying about what others might think. It also tends to heighten people's abilities as their usual human senses are being limited.

The lady began by saying that she saw a dead baby, cancer and blood. She went on to describe a little blonde boy, felt a man in Spirit among some other information regarding a house. This information was said fairly directly and with little understanding of its meaning however the student was following instruction. At this point in development for a student, I am focussed on them being able to receive the information, educating about ethics and delivery as we go. Other people in the group took this information as a negative reflection and judged this lady harshly even labelling her 'dark'. No amount of explaining on my part that this is how mediumship works could change their judgemental thoughts. I tried to explain that I could quite rightly receive the same pictures and the same information in the same way with the only difference being that I have the education and experience to deliver it in the appropriate way.

Even as I explained that the man in Spirit had a blood related cancer, who acknowledged a baby in spirit and was watching over the little boy and that this was all that they were studying to learn, no amount of explaining could save that group. The young lady never returned after feeling so judged and I don't blame her. Talking with her after, she did see the higher purpose in the experience and in my opinion walked away with her dignity.

The rest of the group quickly broke down as I revisited the situation next class and tried to highlight where their judgement and lack of understanding played a role. With a resistance to see this and take some responsibility through their own fears the class finished up fairly quickly as I soon chose not to continue any form of working relationship with the owners who were the main instigators.

When delivering information and offering insight to another, we should never become complacent or forget the responsibility we have with the work. We are often speaking on behalf of another soul as a medium and each medium, whether they realise it or not represents not just other mediums but they also represent the Spirit world, and it is quite easy to get it wrong, misunderstand and cause irrepairable damage. Most people having a negative experience will not just turn away from the psychic involved but they will most likely apply blame across the whole industry with thoughts like *"they're all the same"* and *"they're all fake"* which also means, more importantly they could turn away from searching out their own journey with Spirit.

So how do we work towards understanding the information that comes through. Here, I am offering you my top tips to developing your own understandings and sharing with you some of my personal symbolism to assist you with building a vocabulary of meaning.

1. Work towards having a strong sense of self. Understanding who you are within and honouring it allows a clear distinction between

you and that of the Spirit of another. A good medium also has a thorough understanding of their strengths, weaknesses and limitations as a medium, and it is in knowing oneself that this understanding lies.

2. Know that when communicating with a loved one in Spirit they communicate literally, where as a spirit guide or other spiritual being will communicate symbolically. E.g if a loved one shows you a red car they literally mean a red car, while receiving it from a spirit guide a red car will symbolise your physical journey.

3. Keep a journal specifically to house a record of your developing symbolism. This will help with confidence and clarity helping you to move along, understanding the language of the soul a little more easily.

4. There is one book I recommend every new student of Spirit to read. *Signposts by Denise Linn,* is a book I have been recommending since 1996 when I first read it, and used it to begin understanding how the universe was whispering to me. Since then, many of my students have also used it to great success.

5. Interpreting your messages and understanding the language of the soul is specific to you and your symbolism can be applied across all areas of communicating on a soul level. I use the same language and symbolism I use to communicate with Spirit to also interpret dreams, meditations and external signs. Your signs and symbols will incorporate all of these areas if not more.

Lastly, here I share with you some of the symbolism I work with to help you gain an understanding of how it works and to also help you begin developing your own unique vocabulary and meaning. This is not a complete list and nor should your list ever be complete. It is a work in progress as we are, which means that as we grow and evolve, so to should the language of our soul.

Symbol	Meaning
Spirit stands on my left	Maternal/Wife/Female connection to recipient
Spirit stands on my right	Paternal/Husband/Male connection to recipient
Teddy Bear	Child
Birthday Cake	Birthday
Birthday Cake being pushed forward	Current Birthday
Balloons	Party Celebration
Dove	Anniversary of a passing
Daffodil (Australian specific)	Cancer
Head scarf on female	Cancer with hair loss
Blue flashing lights	Police
Red flashing lights	Ambulance
Red Cross sign	Health issue needing attention
Flags of countries	Related country
Fireworks	4th of July
Australian flag	Australia Day - Jan 26th

Briefcase	Work
Body Bag	Passed away at home
House moving from one spot to another	House Move

To finish this chapter off, just remember that interpreting your messages is not as complicated as we often make it. If you receive it, you are capable of understanding it, why would you receive it otherwise.

In this chapter:
- The universe leads us forward consciously through the flow of synchronicity, 'God's lighted pathway' often referred to us co-incidences.
- A prerequisite of communicating with Spirit is having and living with an open heart.
- Communicating with Spirit is a subtle and simple process.
- All communications received from the spirit world are being received through your frame of reference.
- A good medium has a thorough understanding of their strengths, weaknesses and limitations and have a strong sense of self, thus allows clear distinction between yourself and that of the Spirit of another.
- A loved one in Spirit will communicate literally, a guide will communicate symbolically.

Your Spirit Team

> *The art of communicating is not so much about receiving from without, as to really seeing, feeling and receiving from within.*
> ~**Kerrie Wearing.**

Working with Spirit is an integral part of development for any medium as we strive for guidance from a higher source of love and understanding. In so doing your spirit guide's role is to guide you along a path of spiritual expansion with an ultimate purpose of your personal and soul evolution, while sharing many of the universe's secrets along the way. Actually it is not too different to the role your parents were entrusted with, guiding and assisting you to find your place in this world as you grew and developed into adulthood.

One of the earliest and more exciting connections I made spiritually was that of my first spirit guide. His name was Ralph and my meeting him came about through learning to meditate with some spirit guide meditations at one of the very first metaphysical courses I signed up for. While I didn't complete the course, the repetition of their guided meditation tapes did however open up the connection for me.

Ralph was a medieval monk who symbolically for me, represents the seeker of truth, helping you to find yours by experiencing new learnings. This was a time in my life when I couldn't absorb enough spiritually, reading books, attending groups, workshops, soaking it all up like a sponge and learning as much as I could. Ralph guided me to open up all of this in my life, however looking back connecting with him was more prophetic than I could have imagined at the time. The name Ralph means Wolf Counsel, which at the time I didn't place too much meaning on, now with more knowledge and growth I understand that wolves are the spiritual teachers, providing many things including counsel from the spirit world, which for me today is very much the road I've travelled since those first few meetings with him.

This highlights one of the first things to know and understand about your Spirit team and working with them in a way that helps you achieve your highest potential. Everything has a meaning; however insignificant you may find the message, symbol or sign, Spirit takes great deliberation, thought and preparation in unfolding your spiritual development so for us to deny or not take on anything we receive is letting not just Spirit down, but letting yourself down more so.

I understand that early on, often the communications we receive from Spirit can be quite cryptic and this happens largely for two reasons. Firstly, in the early stages of developing the ability to communicate, we may not be receiving all of the communication which will take care of itself, in time and secondly, we may not hold the knowledge or fully appreciate the personality and culture of our spirit guides.

Quite often you may find yourself working with a guide who hails from a different culture to yours, such as a Native American Indian.

Your relationship and communication with guides such as this can benefit immensely from you honouring their culture and gaining some knowledge of their cultural practices, and an understanding of the way they lived their lives. This opens the door to expand what they can say to you in numerable ways. Think of it as trying to understand someone important to you who does not speak the same language as you. It then becomes our job to find out what they are trying to express and gain some understanding from that.

Let's clarify even a little further. For instance, let's say during your meditation you were given a rock (not a crystal) or even just a leaf. To us, we initially may think these seemingly insignificant items do not make a whole lot of sense. However, if we seek out the possibilities of symbolism, then there could be a variety of meanings. The rock may represent Mother Earth or strength, with your guides trying to communicate that they are your rock. Now the leaf could be for medicinal purposes and we would certainly comprehend more if we had some knowledge of plant life and herbs. Do you see what I'm getting at yet? I'm not suggesting you run out and study botany, but I would suggest that when working with spirit guides of a different culture to your own or an animal guide with their own set of behavioural traits, it pays to invest some time in research to understand your Guide and where they are coming from a little more.

I find that when working and living with Spirit guidance, especially early in development, that my life is more in the flow of harmony and balance then if I try to work at it alone. The magic can unfold in ways you least expect, if we can learn to step outside of ourselves and leave it up to Spirit. There is however, a fine line between allowing the flow of Spirit and using your spirit guide as a crutch instead of taking personal responsibility.

To explain this let us begin by delving into how spirit guides come about. Are they really with us from the moment we are born. Yes and no would be the appropriate answer here. We are all born with spiritual energies of guidance connecting us to the divine which house a knowingness, contain consciousness and connect us all as one. Residual energy left behind in haunted locations or associated with homes and objects is just one aspect of this energy. For those of us that hold a belief and intention rooted in the afterlife and other worlds, this energy can manifest itself in the form of a spirit guide.

Consider those that live and guide themselves with more Eastern based philosophies, or those with Christian beliefs. They all connect and use the same spiritual energies for guidance, just in their own unique way, with the energies having manifested through inner guidance in a way that is right for them not with a spirit guide, as we know them to be seen.

Putting your beliefs in the afterlife, together with your intention to work with a spirit guide, will have your spiritual energies respond in a way that is right for you. It is your intention that sends out the call for this need to be addressed. Reading this book is speaking volumes about your intention. Even just a genuine thought or curiosity is often enough to spur those spiritual energies, or more specifically the spiritual consciousness associated with your own soul group to come together and decide which energy or guide is best suited to your energy and your needs at this present time. It is the consciousness and wisdom with your soul group's spiritual energies that manifest as your spirit guides so we have a tool to work with to assist us in unfolding our spiritual evolution. This process may or may not involve your higher self, it is different for everyone though always based on the intended purpose of your current life cycle.

Coming from your soul group indicates not only have these energies been with you since birth, but perhaps many lifetimes. More importantly, for the here and now this also indicates that you and your spirit guides are aspects of a whole and therefore aspects of one another.

Allow me to use a descriptive analogy to clarify for you. Imagine, if you will a delicious chocolate cake. Mud cake, mmm my favourite! This whole cake, we'll call your soul group, consisting of energies which make up your soul family. You in the now, you long ago, you in the future, family members past and present, all energies associated with your creation and purpose in this life time. Including the consciousness' of your spirit guides. Once the cake has been cut into pieces, we then have individual slices; you, your guides and so forth. Each slice is beautiful and delicious in its own right, revealing secrets as to what lies within the centre of the cake. Not too different to an expression for each individuals life purpose to reveal secrets as to what is at the core of each of us. Life has a way of making this known and your guides are here to assist in that purpose.

Yet, they too have their own individual needs being met. As both of your energies come together, the needs of the evolution of your spirit guide is taken into account as well. Perhaps there is retribution to be made on their behalf which can be achieved by serving another, or compensation to be made by giving their all to you. This is not really a concern for you when working day to day with your spirit guide, however it is beneficial to be mindful of the fact that they have needs to and you are assisting in that journey. It is through this connection of a common purpose that all relationships are formed whether of this world or the world of Spirit.

Your relationship with your spirit guide is by far an extremely personal one, rooted in the understanding of making you whole again, to help you to remember you are a loving being of light created in the image of the Divine. Your spirit guide is an aspect of you and thereby knowing your guide, you are also learning to know yourself. Once your fully know and understand this aspect of you making it a deeper part of who you truly are, the need for the current spirit guide entity ceases to exist. It is at this point of enlightenment that their energy will integrate with yours, becoming a part of the whole again in this life time and other associated energies connected between the two of you, like a ripple. Hearing this, I beg you to ask yourself the question "How well do you know yourself and how well do you know your spirit guide?"

You may find another spirit guide will step forward to guide and assist you along the next phase of your path of evolution, so celebrate at this point, for your growth is the aim and you have just reached a milestone. You can be sure that a lot of hard work went into achieving that milestone, so please take some time to reflect, acknowledge how far you have come and celebrate.

I do need to point out that this process of integration is quite different from one spirit guide saying goodbye and walking away or just not being there anymore to communicate with. Integration feels like coming home and is recognised on a soul level, where these other departures indicate that we got off the train a little too early. Perhaps even needing some respite from the process of conscious spiritual evolution, not fully reaching the destination, stopping short of achieving the full potential of the growth and learning.

For the purpose of mediumship, working with a spirit guide can help and assist immensely in the process of communicating with the spirit world. Saying that though, not everyone will connect with a spirit guide no matter how hard one might try. In these instances, the individuals connection and guidance is one based solely in their higher self. Which is just as powerful and valuable, if not more so for the purpose of evolution. Our higher self is that part of us directly connected to the Divine which means the guidance and information we receive through this channel is of the same source that a spirit guide will offer their guidance from. Yet there is a great sense of valuing your own wisdom, and the personal responsibility to be gained that comes with this type of connection, instead of developing a crutch like relying solely on your spirit guide. So if you find no spirit guide manifests for you, yet you receive guidance and wisdom, know that this is not wrong in any way. It is just what works best for you. Embrace it and trust in yourself.

Over the years most of my knowledge into the technical workings of mediumship has been learnt through experience, and then coming back to my guides or now my higher self and asking for an explanation. If something didn't go well or work out as I expected I spent a lot of time referring to and working with Spirit on these technicalities. I recall when I first stepped out to work publicly with evidential mediumship in a gallery setting, I encountered an experience which nearly stopped me in my tracks. It was only my third mediumship demonstration and was with a lovely bunch of ladies, some of whom had seen me work previously on a night which was far more successful than this night proved to be. I stood there receiving information but not being able to place it. One piece of information would make sense for one person only to have the next piece relate to someone else. The information was all over the place and I couldn't get it together. I felt terrible! On the night I returned the ladies their money and we ended up just enjoying a chat. Spirit could not have provided a more supportive group of women for me to go through that experience with. No matter how great they were though, I was devastated!

This was at a time when mediumship teaching was not how it is these days. I didn't have a teacher or mentor who understood the technicalities. I did however, have a friend, another medium who was so supportive encouraging me to get back on the horse. His support helped me to turn around my state of mind and once clear of the emotion, I referred it to Spirit asking *"What had happened?"* My team showed me that it was about needing to gain some control over the energies and the Spirit communicators I was working with. Imagine walking into a room full of people all trying to communicate all at once and not being fully aware of that. If the medium isn't able to take some control and assert themselves by asking for one communicator at a time, then it can be very confusing for everyone, including the audience. Asserting control in this instance can be as simple as recognising this is happening and asking them all to step back while one Spirit person steps forward at a time. You might think, why doesn't this happen naturally anyway. We are dealing with energy and sometimes the Spirit world may not be aware of how the medium is receiving the energies. They may not be aware of any confusion, if the medium is not aware of it. Hence, it is our responsibility to understand and improve situations such as this. In time, the mediums energy adjusts and masters these effects with awareness and training, though in the beginning most mediums new to demonstrating will experience something similar. I learnt to expect this lesson for my students, which meant I was quickly on hand with the benefit of my hindsight, so they did not experience the shock and devastation as I did.

This began my quest for knowledge and understanding of the intricacies regarding the mechanics behind mediumship. There have been many such learning opportunities, some as painful as this one, but most not so. Some have even been laughable, like the time I was driving to another home demonstration and while preparing, Spirit told me *"It's ok to ask questions."* I thought they were saying that it was ok for the gathering of people to ask me and Spirit questions. Well it wasn't until the next day that I had the realisation *"Oh Kerrie, you nutter. They meant for me to ask Spirit questions"*. Questions such as *"Can I have your name please?"* And *"how old where you when you passed?"* This was changing old habits for me as for many years I'd been taught to just sit and receive. Yet again, a little slow on the up take.

Understanding the workings behind your mediumship is vital for any medium working with integrity. The onus is on us to understand why we can or cannot make it work, or why we can read for one person but not another. Where do our own ego and limitations get in the way, and if you think they don't then you need to think again. We need to take responsibility for not being able to read well through blockages such as grief, high expectations, judgement and the like. Not knowing how these energies affect your ability to read and just passing blame to Spirit, or worse still to the recipient is not acceptable. Believe me, it does happen. Many clients have told of previous negative experiences like this, and yes most of these clients have challenging energies to work with, though with understanding, integrity and acknowledgement they can be managed.

It is your Spirit team that can help you understand all of this, so that you can grow into a medium who truly stands for knowledge, integrity and love. Allowing your Spirit team to have a greater voice, not just in the area of your mediumship development but also in your life will see your personal life change in ways you least expect. Coming from your heart space and aligning it with your mind through the function of a Spirit Guide will see your awareness expand, your heart heal and life begin to become more of what you want it to be. This process does not happen overnight, in fact it can take years. Though by working with Spirit, that is your own Spirit and that of the Spirit world you are giving yourself the best chance to become the high potential of the true you, with a life that reflects this.

A loving being of light, you already are. But do you see it, do you live your life knowing this. Let Spirit guide you to that.

Spirit Guide Meditation

With your feet flat on the floor, close your eyes gently taking a deep breath in through the nose and out through the mouth. With each breath, I want you to focus on asking your body to relax as you visualise a beautiful rose quartz pink energy filling the room.

This energy starts to find its way up through your feet and into your body. First you start to feel it surging through your feet and calves, as they tingle and start to feel warm.

It then slowly moves along to the tops of your legs relaxing you further. On the next breath the pink energy reaches your torso filling you with a warm upper body glow as you exhale.

On further still, the soft pink energy finds its way up into your head – where it brings peace and tranquility as you find your mind now, surprisingly quiet. With this, the energy then weaves its way out of your body through the top of your head and your crown chakra, rejoining the beautiful pink light of energy that abounds in your room.

Peacefully take three more deep breaths, in through the nose and out through the mouth. As you do you find yourself relaxing further and further into your chair.

Amidst the pink energy in your room, a scene starts to unfold before you; this energy slowly gives way to a beautiful clear sunny day with a magnificent garden where all you can see are a vast array of flowers and abundant growth. Don't they smell divine! You are quite taken with the beauty that abounds here. Take a moment to enjoy your surrounds.

In the distance on top of a gentle rolling slope, you see a big beautiful old oak tree. This tree is steeped in history, it has seen many changes over time and many people come and go. Today this tree and all its glory is there for you.

As you look down at your feet, you suddenly become aware of the path you are standing on. The dirt beneath your feet is the very path that leads to the tree. As you begin to step forward, you notice you are not alone. Beside you are these beautiful shimmering lights like you never seen before, dancing all about you. You have a strong sense that these lights are important, almost as if they can whisper sweet secrets in your ear.

Taking another step forward you become aware of your heart beating. At first it seems quite soft but with each step it is becoming more noticeable, beating in time with every step you take, ba boom, ba boom, ba boom.

Soon you notice that your shimmering lights are vibrating as well. You ask yourself, is that right? Can they be pulsating in time with your heart beat? Of course is the answer as you have a sense that this feels divinely perfect.

With each step, the sense of connection between you and these Spirit lights is strengthening as both hearts beat as one, ba boom, ba boom, ba boom.

Finally you come upon your tree, and as you do, turning to look at the lights you find they are no longer lights, they have materialized into an old friend, someone you feel like you have known for quite a long time.

Under the shade of the tree, take some time to let your spirit guide share with you a little something of themselves. They may share in many ways. Notice how you are feeling, are you hearing thoughts from long ago, or do you see what it is they would like you to know.

Enjoy some time for further meditation 10 – 15mins should suffice.

As the sun starts to set and the day is nearing its end, your new old friend is preparing to make leave, but before they do they have a gift for you. Something of themselves they give you. Hold this close for keepsakes.

With a deep sense of gratitude say goodbye for now to your spirit guide, thanking them for the sharing today. As you turn to travel back down the path from whence you came, please remember to thank the tree for its presence and gifts as well.

Coming back along the path, you return with a strong sense of never having to be alone again. Always knowing your friend is there whenever you may need them. Slowly as you get further along the path to where you began, the garden slowly starts to fade with your awareness returning to the room you are sitting in. You slowly start to become aware of your body, in your own time opening your eyes.

Tip: *May I suggest, you make a recording of this meditation. Read it out loud at a slow and gentle pace with ten to fifteen second pauses between each step. This will enable you to relax more within the meditation, allowing the energies and your guides to work their charm.*

Congratulations! I sincerely hope that this meditation was a gift from Spirit for you. To those of you that may have struggled, please persevere as I know from experience and working with many students that we all get there eventually. If you are inexperienced at meditating then it may take a little longer to reap the benefits. It will come, I assure you.

In this chapter:
- When a guide presents itself to you, being of human or animal kind, invest some time to research your guide to help you understand their culture and behavioural traits which will further expand your ability to communicate with them.
- Your spirit guide is as much a part of you as you are of them, with your energies working together for your own growth and their evolution as well.
- A spirit guide can help a medium immensely when making connections to communicate with the spirit world.
- Many mediums connect with their higher self to bring mediumship information through.

Developing Your New Talent

> *Love and magic have a great deal in common.*
> *They enrich the soul, delight the heart.*
> *And they both take practice.*
> **~Nora Roberts.**

It is through listening to one's own Spirit that the gift of communicating with those in the afterlife develops springing forth from the well of wisdom within you. In preparing this chapter I initially planned to cover the use of some of the more popular psychic tools. However, after encountering a blockage and finally taking the time to listen to my own Spirit, what sprang forward was the importance of conveying to you, how imperative it is to listen within and hear the inner wisdom and let it guide you.

It is from this basis that you build and connect to the energies around you, be it the energies of other people, the afterlife or the collective universal energies. Here you make the first steps to ground yourself, finding your place in this universe and begin to understand where you begin and end. This all assists you to grow in your own personal power while learning to hear clearly the whisperings of Spirit as their communications traverse through the universal ether.

My own techniques to listen to the voice within are varied, though what is common is the fact that I am in touch consciously with my inner self on a daily basis. Hearing it speak, gently nudging me in one direction or another, take action in a certain way, to be in service for someone if need be, to be more aware as a parent or partner and to honour my own Spirit above all this and the daily grind of the rat race. Sharing with you a couple of my favourite techniques which will I hope, inspire you to communicate daily with your inner self, giving it a voice and allowing that part of you to guide you forth.

Getting the most out of Journaling

Journaling is the process of writing about your thoughts, experiences and emotions on a regular basis. I find this process immensely beneficial and will use it to clarify confusion, heal emotion, to receive guidance and communicate with Spirit including my own Spirit and those in the Spirit world. Its potential is unlimited and therefore only limited by undervaluing what it can do for you.

It is always nice to write in a beautiful journal selected for the specific purpose of your private musings. So spoil yourself a little and buy yourself a nice journal.

To begin with, regularly set aside some time each day to journal. Developing a habit will be of benefit and discovering which time of day works best for you will also help. Whether it be in the morning, when you are fresh and can enjoy the mornings' crisp newness of the day with a cup of tea, or if you prefer the quietness of the evening once everyone is in bed it is completely up to you. Over time you'll find that with a habit developed you will be able to relax your routine and will yourself readily able to journal at any given moment, as your soul understands what is to come and springs forth eager to offer itself to you.

- Find a nice quiet space to sit and write, somewhere where you won't be disturbed for a few minutes. With journal and pen in hand, center yourself by taking a few deep breaths and focusing your awareness within your heart space. Certainly, if a few minutes of a meditation helps to do this, then by all means enjoy a meditation.
- Begin writing with the words… *"I am here to seek the inner voice within. It is I, Kerrie (insert your name) who seeks communication with my soul within. I listen and will honour this gift by acting accordingly. Please speak now."*
- At this point write whatever comes to your mind. Do not censor it, analyse it or try to understand it. Keep the flow going by just writing all that comes forth.
- As you write, feel free to introduce a question by writing it down. Questioning, your inner source will help you to clarify anything you need to further understand and can be extremely helpful when it comes to seeking guidance on how to proceed with a specific situation.
- Exhaust your connection by continuing to write until you feel a sense of completion. Sign off with some words of thanks and gratitude and just sit for a moment to soak it all in.

Journaling is the tool I enjoy and prefer above most being that I love to write, and I do find the guidance and information I can glean totally invaluable. Whether I am working through fear or an emotional blockage, to marketing and business guidance this technique always provides the goods.

Your Intuitive Navigation System

Described on Page 107, in the chapter on *Understanding your Spiritual Abilities'*, this technique is one that I recommend should be developed and integrated so much that it becomes a natural part of who you are, giving you a powerful tool to use in each and every moment.

Beginning by laying a foundation based in daily connection with Spirit begins building a bridge for further communication. As you hear the whispers from the Spirit world you will know and understand whether the information you are receiving is from yourself or from another soul. You will learn how your framework of knowledge, your limitations, your strengths and weaknesses influence the information you receive, thereby giving you a greater possibility to step outside of yourself, be objective and operate with a much clearer channel with Spirit. Hearing yourself relay your experiences regularly to your recipients is one way of knowing that there is too much of you in the process, if this is happening time and time again, especially if this relates to one particular experience. At this time, I suggest you stop reading for other people and spend some time reflecting and working through some self healing around this issue for yourself.

Another indicator of not being in Spirit is feeling the need to banish any negative Spirits and energies away. I delve more deeply into this topic in the next chapter but for now know that Spirit operates on a level of love without judgement and offering greater understanding. Therefore any energy you come in contact with lies in an experience which can offer you a greater understanding of yourself, so any information or experience other than this indicates too much humanness, judgement, fear and ego. Sure its ok to be cautious but to rid one's soul of a connection to another soul does not reflect an awareness or understanding of the fact that we are all connected as one and created from the same source. Sure, there is darkness but there must also be light which can only be found if we look for it.

Integrity begins in the heart of a person and cannot be given, if its not there. We can educate and raise someone's awareness but the choice to do the right thing comes naturally from within. With this in mind here are my thoughts on providing mediumship with a high integrity.

Let's begin by conducting a reading
- Begin by asking if your recipient is new to the process or has experienced a spirit communication before. Recently, I have also taken to asking what they want to achieve from our time together, i.e. are they wanting a Spirit communication (I do not ask who at this point) or do they want me to focus on guidance for their life. It is a good idea at this point to explain how you work the process so they know what to expect.
- Personally, I explain that I prefer everything to flow of its own fruition first. This way I allow the process which works on a soul level and Spirit to set the priority of what needs to be discussed. This can sometimes be different to what we consciously want, hence the saying *"You always get what you need, not necessarily what you want."* Secondly, the recipient is not feeding the psychic with information or directing in anyway what comes through.
- I explain that I will ask questions, however these questions are designed to gauge the fact that the recipient is relating to the information coming through. i.e. Does this make sense to you? Can you relate to this? Do you understand?

    Should you need to ask a question to clarify the information you are receiving, for example, you have received the name Fred, but do not know if they are living or in the afterlife? Ask this question to Spirit, not your recipient. Asking your recipient is lazy mediumship, when it really is our job to build the story with the help of Spirit. Work towards minimising how many questions are asked of your recipient. Directing your questions to Spirit instead of your recipient also makes it harder for a skeptic to accuse you of cold reading.
- Lastly, I advise that I will allow time for their questions and

answers towards the end. This includes if someone they are looking to connect with specifically hasn't come through of their own fruition or what they want covered about their life has not come up for discussion either. Most times, what the client wants covered is taken care of naturally, though I do want my clients to receive all that they are looking for, and this format allows me to balance this need with need of Spirit.

As the information begins to flow, I am very conscious of ensuring that the information I am receiving and providing them with relates for them wholeheartedly, and I work very hard to ensure that this happens very early on in the reading. Should they not relate or it doesn't feel as if the information is hitting home, I will halt the reading early on and offer their money back.

Yes we could argue that perhaps it is information they may not want to hear, or that perhaps the information will be validated later on and these are valid points. However, I do believe that these points can and will only be a component of a reading, not all of it. A good reading with integrity will always contain information that your client can relate to in the moment, and working towards engaging that in the beginning of a session establishes your credibility with your client which allows the energies to flow more openly. This helps you to receive information more readily and sets things up so you can manage the reading professionally should it not be happen quite how you like it.

As we turn our attention to the information and content of a reading, there is one rule above all else which we need to bare in mind. The saying *"All care, no responsibility"* does not apply here. While we receive information from Spirit and what comes through is what comes through, we really do not have a right to censor it. However, how we deliver the information and its affect on the recipient is our responsibility.

Many times I have heard the story about how without explanation a psychic couldn't read someone, or stopped a reading not wanting to go any further leaving the recipient fearing the worst. This is totally unprofessional and inappropriate. If a psychic can't deal with the information or what is before them, then they shouldn't be using their abilities to offer information to other people.

I often get asked how to I deal with information which is of a negative nature, such as if I receive information about when someone is going to pass away or if someone is at risk of harm. For me there is no rule of thumb, as each and every situation is different. Though if I receive it, I am going to pass it on, usually in some way with a little discretion. I recall a situation quite a few years ago where I was working publicly during a demonstration, and began by describing the appearance of man for a lady in the audience. She identified him as her husband's best friend. I then described a little boy (her son) and saw the man enticing the boy with a lolly coupled with feeling that this little boy was at risk of child abuse. However, I did not come out directly and make this accusation. Firstly, from Spirit's perspective this man could have been only having these thoughts and not acted on them, which is very difficult for Spirit to communicate the difference. Secondly, there are the legal ramifications we need to keep in mind. So I said to her, *"I don't like this man and if that was my son I would be supervising contact at all times"*. Enough said for all to understand.

Writing this, reminds of the time when a friend was demonstrating many years ago and another psychic was sitting in the audience. At the end of the night the psychic sitting in the audience jumped up and said they had clairvoyantly seen a car accident and people needed to be careful driving home, thus as you can imagine creating some fear. My friend disagreed with this and explained that what was more likely to be happening was this psychic was connecting with a Spirit who had passed in a car accident, only to be inexperienced at survival evidence mediumship even though they were a working psychic professional.

Bare in mind your limitations, your knowledge and be honest with where you are at in your own journey. Your clients deserve it, and more importantly so too does the Spirit world and the industry you may represent.

In 2005, I visited the Learning Light Foundation in Anaheim, California which provided me with the inspiration to established ACOM. During that visit, I had a more personal experience while attending a Spirit circle there with a well known medium from the UK. There were only a handful of us in attendance and this medium was a regular visitor to the center, having appeared on TV and had been widely accepted as having been in contact with Princess Diana. We all received readings to which we all related and you could not fault her evidence or question whether she was making a link.

However, what did lack was the most important ingredient of any reading, and for me it was this experience which taught me how important it is. Her delivery of the information did not come from Spirit or a place of love. All of it lacked empathy, understanding or helping her clients to receive healing. To the lady next to me she flat out said *"Why aren't you divorced yet?"* and then proceeded to go on about it. This lady told me later that she did have her divorce papers in the glove box of the car but was finding it difficult to action. Surely the medium could have empowered her there. To the lady on the other side of me she said *"Your dad (in Spirit) is not happy that you haven't received your inheritance"* and placed a lot of guilt on this ladies shoulders. When the lady shared she was being deceived by her brother in another country, the medium only reiterated and did not offer any assistance in the way of how to help the situation. To me, she connected with my brother and said that I was mean to him, always hitting and picking on him, that I should be sorry for it all and got away with far too much. When I questioned her, saying *"Hang on a minute, he got away with far more than I did*" Her response was *"That's because your parents knew what you were doing"*. I described early on in this book, how I was parented and that this lead to my parenting my brother the same way from the age of eleven. I did and still do to some extent carry guilt about this, but I know my brother and Spirit. He would have been far more likely been trying to convey *"Don't worry about it Kez, let it go. We know what we went through and I love you."* In this instance, the mediums own issue with guilt affected her link with Spirit and her delivery was unacceptable.

This experience did highlight for me the importance of healing and empowerment in a reading. That every single time when one sits before a medium, if the connection is truly coming from Spirit and not ego, then the experience of love, understanding and growth will be felt, therefore its imperative a medium is also living from the space of love. Once, I received the inspiration for ACOM that same year, it became my mission to ensure those I taught became aware and attained this level of integrity to be able to spread the same word through their own work. It was then I developed the ACOM mediumship criteria.

All facets of a mediumship communication can be categorised into one of three categories with each of these categories having their own purpose, yet when they come together as a whole the effect is a well rounded, powerful connection with Spirit.

Spirit Identification

This category is by far the easiest and most logical category to include. Easy because, if you watch a lot of mediumship by a variety of mediums, this information flows through relatively easy. Even developing mediums in their first year can receive this information quite well. So if your psychic claims a link to Spirit but is not able to provide any of the following to prove it is your loved one, then I would be asking for my money back.

- Appearance descriptions

- Personality characteristics
- Career
- Address descriptions
- Names
- Information on how they crossed over
- Relationship

Proof of Consciousness

Aimed at proving our loved ones still exist and are connected to us in the moment, this category and receiving its information consistently is much harder to achieve for fear of being wrong. Telling your recipient that their dad saw them buy a new necklace or that he appreciated the fact you played his favourite music to him as he lay in hospital passing away, are the moments where the magic happens yet it takes a lot of work for a medium to become practiced and experienced at receiving information such as this.

For me personally, once the Spirit has been identified well, I look forward to seeing the proof of consciousness information. Too much about the Spirit can get a little boring when watching someone demonstrate, however when watching the proof come through that they are still with us and can acknowledge new members of the family, that recent pay rise or the fact they know someone in the family has had some ill health proves without a doubt that their Spirit and consciousness not only exists after death, but they are still part of our lives. Magic!

- Information predominately about the living which has occurred since the passing of the Spirit (i.e., not just memories you have).
- Recently moved house/changed jobs/had a baby etc
- Names and acknowledgements about the living
- Daily events of all sorts for example celebrations, decorating, speeding tickets etc

- Significant details regarding funerals, jewellery, spirit visitations etc.
- Birthdays, Anniversaries etc.

Message of Healing

This category rounds it all out and connects to the purpose of the reading. It taps into the underlying spiritual need of all parties and answers such questions as to why you hear from a particular Spirit today instead of the one you want to, or why your loved ones need to say something completely unexpected. Hearing they are supporting you through difficult times and they understand your decision to leave your partner, or that Grandpa has the wisdom, knowledge and experience you need right now; to Grandma, who keeps coming in your dreams because its time to awaken your spiritual abilities. These messages of healing all work towards leading the recipient to greater understandings, so that in recognising the spirit of their loved one, they recognise their own Spirit and its connection to the Divine.

I have often said to my beginner students over the years that this is not really a category I can teach you. The ability to work towards facilitating healing for someone else lies in how well you do that for yourself. If self healing and striving to achieve your own personal growth and new levels of understanding are not at the core of your spirituality and who you are as a person, then it is going to be very difficult to achieve healing for others with your mediumship.

Mediumship which lacks this aspect will find that the information coming through is often repetitive, monotonous and succinctly just facts – lacking any real feeling. The depths that are needed to be reached within one's own soul to effect a brilliant mediumship communication will be given over to operating from one's own ego, surface level stuff. Still quite effective in its own way, yet missing the true Spirit essence and not felt by the recipient enough to effect deep change within them. Heal your own heart first and this category will become a natural instinct.

Measuring all of this information is the basis for my Mediumship certification program and it stands to reason that when we question whether a medium is effective at the work they do. We only need look at the quality of information and their approach in their work to recognise whether they are good at what they do and more importantly whether they deserve you trusting them with your heart and hard earned money as one of my clients Laura found recently.

Laura's Story

Laura is a developing medium whom I have been privately coaching and working with over the last year. During that time we've grown quite fond of one another and I truly admire the kind of truth, integrity and professionalism she brings to her work.

As is the nature of working with Spirit, your personal life is heavily entwined in developing and progressing your Mediumship which for Laura lies in understanding more about her father and his family while also moving through the physical and emotional challenges which present when trying to conceive a baby with IVF.

Laura came to me recently for the specific purpose of having a Mediumship reading which began with her husband's grandmother coming through followed by her father. Having mentioned little details such that Grandma had three children and always wore knee-hi stockings, and that Lesley and her dad share the same round face, gave Laura the confidence to trust in what was to come through for the purpose of healing. Her willingness to open up and self-heal made this an easy process for me.

Grandma stepped forward specifically out of all of Laura's Spirit family to love and support Laura and her husband in regard to the current set of fertility issues. Grandma shared that this was her experience too and she fully understood how painful it could be. So she stepped forward to help and support however she can. As you can imagine this was immensely beneficial on many levels for Laura to hear, and here in her own words is the feedback she shared with me after.

"I can't believe how emotional I felt during the reading, I could hear it in my voice, but what is even more amazing is that since the reading I have felt a sense of contentment, almost like I've eaten a good meal and it's sitting comfortably in my tummy and I don't want for any more.

You know Kerrie, up until my reading with you I kept on searching, I felt empty and at times frustrated. I've had four mediumship readings this past year, you were number five and even though I left feeling disillusioned at some people's abilities at times, I didn't mind spending the money as I had learned a great deal about mediumship and about how I didn't want to work.

But I realised something different after my reading with you, I realised just how much it truly meant to get that validation and really understand that there is a meaning and purpose as to why they (spirit) come through and connect; not just theoretically, but how it felt on an emotional level, I truly get it now and I learnt that from you Kerrie and strive to be that way myself.

I thank my father for sending me on that mission to find that right medium for my own spiritual evolvement and healing so that I will be able to, in time, share that privilege with others."

When developing your Mediumship, be conscious of striving to receive information that is relevant with a higher purpose for coming through. Why that piece of information as opposed to another? Why this Spirit instead of someone else? Work with your spirit guides or higher self to bring it about. I recall very early on being able to describe the Spirit appearance, which made sense for the recipient however, I wasn't satisfied and wanted more. I wanted to know who were they, mum, dad or grandma. So I sat down with my journal and outlined with my spirit guide the kinds of information I wanted to see coming through, i.e. how they passed, names, relationships and so forth. After this at the very next demonstration I did, I started to receive their relationship right from the very first reading of the night. Exciting! These days of course, I'm not so controlling, however I still advise you to recognise the partnership that exists between you and your spirit team. Work with them in ways such as this and together strive for good quality, credible information with a strong conscious intention to work towards healing, always.

In this chapter:
- Regular journaling greatly assists with clarifying confusion, healing emotion, receiving guidance and communication with Spirit.
- Creating a foundation based in daily connection with Spirit builds a bridge for more communication.
- When receiving information from Spirit, we do not have the right to censor it. However, we do have a responsibility in how the information is delivered.
- Healing and empowerment within a reading is of vital importance.

Haunted Access

> *Your experience with the Spirit world is a reflection of you.*
> ~**Kerrie Wearing.**

It would be remiss of me to write this book on mediumship and not include my thoughts on the topic of hauntings and paranormal phenomena, especially seeing that mainstream television is full of a variety of paranormal shows that all pertain to investigate haunted locations and the afterlife. I often think that those in Spirit must be looking down on our efforts and laughing half the time. These shows are designed purely for entertainment, otherwise they wouldn't make it onto TV, yet those with an interest in the paranormal see them as educational. A big mistake in my view, with what mostly has been shown on our screens. Take a trip to any haunted location with a view to investigate and you will find the reality is quite different to what is being portrayed on TV. Couple this with the fact that the vast majority of hauntings are misinterpreted and you will find that we really understand very little about the paranormal and its effects on this world.

My interest in the paranormal and how it is represented began in 2006 when Spirit asked me to arrange a ghost tour for the then students of ACOM to experience their mediumship in an environment outside of the usual development circle setting. I shared earlier in the book that this lead us to Berrima Courthouse and meeting the energy of John Lynch.

There was a time, like most people, that I believed that Spirit exists everywhere and that a haunting occurred when one of these Spirits became trapped between this world and the next causing them to be earthbound. It was in meeting John, that these beliefs were challenged and my mindset became one of working towards breaking down fear and judgement towards this aspect of the Spirit world, usually known as the lower astral plane.

People too easily take the experience of a haunting as something that just happens to them, without seeing or even looking for their responsibility in it. The universal law of like attracts like lies at the heart of every experience we encounter in life, including those experiences which are paranormal by nature. Energy attracts like energy, consciously or unconsciously, and to understand this principal and how it manifests in a haunting, one must look within.

The true nature of a haunting will only be revealed once we take the time to look within ourselves for answers. I have said before that your interactions with the Spirit world are a reflection of you, the law of attraction makes it so. Without allowing room for this principal, any thoughts people have on interpreting a haunting are misconceived until they allow room for a much fuller picture. On top of this, most hauntings are interpreted from the view point of standing in this world and coming to a somewhat one sided theory. To be objective and try to gain a fuller understanding of a haunting, we need to try and step out of our humanness and view things from a more spiritual perspective;

almost as if we were fully living in the world of Spirit.

Time is the first factor we must try to step out of. In the world of energy there is no time, with time being a manmade construct so we may manage some sort of order out of all the chaos which is humanity. Therefore what we relegate as happening in the here and now of the spirit world relative to our world, really bares no semblance if you wholly existed in the world of energy. Multi dimensional and multi faceted is the world of energy, meaning it can be in this world but not of it. The world of energy can reach through the veil and interact with this world, only seemingly to have its place rooted in this world, which is not necessarily the case. We only view it to be so, because we are looking at it from our humanness and standing in this world.

Imagine if your view was from a much higher perspective, one where you saw everything from a much greater height, giving you a wider view of all that is involved. A bird's eye view if you will. From this vantage point, you would see how the coming together of the two worlds could cause disturbances for all involved, only for these interactions to be misunderstood or how one world is oblivious to the other.

Take the prime example of a ghost, we may interpret as repeatedly acting out a set of circumstances continually, seeming unaware that they are dead and therefore not aware of this world. If we remember that time doesn't exist where they are, it begs the question are they really repeating or has a touching of the two worlds synchronised in such a way to give off this impression. If a ghost is not aware they are dead, then perhaps in their world they aren't. Their alternate reality exists and operates along side of ours and perhaps in their life, their death hasn't occurred yet relative to the moment in time we are connecting with. Some Spirits even may be fully aware and interacting with this world could still have a basis of living in a thriving alternate reality.

At the beginning of 2007, I visited an abandoned health facility in the Blue Mountains of NSW along with a paranormal investigation group I did a little bit of work with at the time. This facility, was one of the most foreboding places I have ever visited. To this day, I have never felt the feeling of death like that existed in this old hospital. Coming home at three am in the morning, I stopped in my driveway to cleanse and smudge my aura prior to going in the house, to bed next to my husband. It was quite yucky!

This facility was known to house some mental health patients and I received an insight to say that the land contained a body pit, which was confirmed by the investigation group. The group of investigators had previously seen an apparition of a matron walking down the corridor carrying towels or sheets. On this visit while completing our walk through, we found that a couple of patients in Spirit began to follow us around and I heard them clairaudiently say "They can see us." Once we sat down in a vigil and I had time to focus and communicate with the energies, I connected with a doctor who explained that he conducted lobotomies for research purposes. I felt that his intentions were honourable and truly because he believed he was furthering science. This explained the body pit a little and I came to understand that the energies presented as an alternate reality that existed in this location. In this other dimension, it was still a fully functioning mental health facility and we were encroaching on their world. Some of the experiences, such as the matron walking down the corridor still working, validated this theory and leaves you to wander who really is haunting who. About two am, the matron had obviously had enough of us intruding when she made herself know with a stereophonic moment of heavy breathing and sparking an electro-magnetic frequency (EMF) detector, an electronic device which measures EMF, all while we were sitting in pitch black dark and couldn't see our own hand in front of us.

Opening our minds to a broader set of understandings in turn opens up the possibilities. To my mind, seeing any Spirit, no matter how 'negative' they may be as earthbound, just does not sit well with me. I believe that we are all created in the likeness of our Creator and there exists a light within each and every one of God's creations. Once we leave this world, I honestly believe that we have our own natural place in the light of the afterlife. Yes, this light may be diminished for some due to their hurt, pain and lack of understanding, we all experience that at times. But for me to say another soul is not of the light is too big a judgement for me to make. Who am I to say, that another soul is stuck in the belief of who they are, anymore than I can say that of you.

Only yesterday, I was working with a client who has been experiencing a haunting with an internationally well known personality. This visitation started off innocent enough after her interest in their passing sparked a connection. She could relate wholeheartedly to their trials, tribulations and pain just as if it were her own. Not realising this link, my client found herself dealing with an attachment that she could not control which was taking over a large part of her private life, affecting her thoughts and emotions dramatically enough for people and herself to question her mental stability. This is certainly one of the first things I look to rule out when helping someone with this kind of situation.

Over the period of approximately nine months, this haunting was growing and turning more and more into a negative experience matched by the negativity now coming from the Spirit. This client came to me desperate, having tried everything to get this Spirit to 'cross over'. Her understanding was that he didn't go into the light because of his anger and resentment towards the way in which he passed and the fact that he didn't want to die. Why this Spirit has seemingly come to my client for help? She didn't know.

Before I begin working with a client to help resolve a situation of this nature, I usually begin by explaining that my beliefs are different than the norm, even somewhat controversial. Hence giving them the choice to accept working with me or not. Here I offer you the same choice. My beliefs and theories shared in this chapter are just that, my beliefs. I share them with you in the hope a part of them may resonate with you, prompting further thought and therefore an expansion of your own belief system. My explanation may not be for all of you, but here it is anyway.

To me this Spirit is not earthbound, nor did it not go to the light. The answer lies in the chocolate cake analogy I used earlier when explaining the composition of the Spirit world. This Spirit has a continuing worldwide reach, just as they did in life and when we make a connection to their energy, we connect to an aspect of their energy or a slice of the chocolate cake. Which aspect do we connect with? That answer lies in the law of attraction and the fact that like energy attracts like energy. This is true in haunted locations as well. Our intention to investigation and connect with the afterlife draws to us like a magnet, the aspects of the energy associated with those souls and their experiences connected to the location. Let's say we have a Spirit we experience in a haunted location, but then a medium communicates with the same Spirit through a reading for a family member. They would be two very different experiences even though it is the one and same Spirit.

As I began to work with my client having explained all of this, she did recognise that the Spirit was feeding off her energy, which is a natural occurance. Interactions from the spirit world cannot exist without the energy of this world. I often use the old analogy "if a tree fell in the woods, with no one to hear it would it still make a sound?" What I did need to explain though, was what her energy was bringing to the equation. Because of not being able to control this energy or have it move on, and not understanding the purpose behind it all happening. My client was getting more and more fearful and it was this energy that was feeding the energy of the Spirit, resulting in the increasing negativity she was experiencing from the Spirit. Leaving this unattended, could eventually see this Spirit manifest even more negatively and eventually present as a demon to this lady.

Once we take the time to look within and delve deep into what it is about our own energy that connects us to the energy of another, in the case of a Spirit attachment we generally find that the answer lies in a common emotional pain. The Spirit attached with my client has some unresolved anger relating to his mother where he felt let down and betrayed by her over a certain situation and this was true for my client and her mother too. This was just the beginning of what together, they needed to work through. For me, this experience had presented at a time when they are both ready to heal this hurt, let it go and accept more love in both of their lives, thereby reaching a new level of enlightenment and growth of the soul. Is this not what the process of 'going to the light' is really all about anyway. Just trying to get this spirit to walk through a doorway of light was never going to work. Taking the time to work with this spirit, learning and growing together can bring about positive life change for all involved.

This process of healing will work every time, even if it takes longer to achieve, and it has a stronger foundation in its outcomes to never reoccur for the same reason, as the healing takes place on a deeper soul level for those involved. Where as some of the usual processes of banishing a Spirit, cleansing and smudging will see the situation reoccur as the underlying energies of attraction have not been addressed. Over the years, I have found this technique and approaching a Spirit attachment in this way has always been effective and insightful for those willing to look within, heal and see their own truth. Many, many of my clients and students have grown to new levels of understanding by working with Spirit in this way. So the next time, you come across a Spirit that makes you a little uncomfortable or you think may be earthbound, I hope that you take some time to question and expand your beliefs a little.

In this chapter:

- What is depicted on TV is very different to reality.
- If experiencing a haunting, you need to be brave and look within yourself and be prepared to work and heal on the aspect of yourself that has attracted the spirit to you, consciously or unconsciously, as like attracts like.
- In the world of energy, there is no time. Time is a manmade construct created by humanity.
- It is possible you are connecting into another alternate reality that co-exists with our reality.

The Psychic Child

> *We cannot fashion our children after our desires,*
> *we must have them and love them as*
> *God has given them to us.*
> ~**Johann Wolfgang von Goethe.**

In the beginning we all commence our human experience intricately entwined with the energy of another. Our time spent in utero with our mother heralds the beginnings of human experience and it is from here that efforts are made to ensure the best possible process of integration occurs for the soul, as it adjusts to the human body, its environment and surrounds including the energy of the family dynamics.

How this is approached, at what point does the soul attach to the body, whether it comes and goes or is fully aligned depends wholeheartedly on the needs and capabilities of the soul. There is no rule of thumb, just a gentle process of integration.

I recall being about eleven or twelve weeks pregnant with my daughter and experiencing some bleeding around this time. With the pregnancy in question, as we worried one morning my then two year old son, Nathan and I were snuggling in bed when he pointed to the corner of the bedroom near the roofline and asked *"What's that?"* I replied *"I don't know, what can you see?"* Nathan responded with *"Santa. Eyes but no mouth."* When I asked him to go close and show me, he said no and exhibited some fear, not wanting to get too close. This was early in the new year, not long after Christmas so for a toddler to liken a white form of energy to that of Santa does make sense and I absolutely believe that what he saw was the soul of my daughter, Jessica coming to hang out with her new family. All part of the integration process needed for her to come into this world.

We all know that many, many children exhibit similar insight and behaviour to that shown by Nathan in the early years of life. You can ask anyone you know and I'm sure they will have a story to share. This in my mind implies recognition that we are a soul first and a human second. On a soul level children easily recognise, more so than adults that we exist in the world of energy first and are born into this physical existence as a likeness and the human expression of who we are as a soul, relevant to the agreements and experiences aligned for this lifetime experience.

Your agreements being those ideal circumstances we agree to prior to incarnating, which are designed to provide us with the greatest potential to help us achieve the evolutionary growth we are aiming to gain from this current lifetime experience. This topic can be a whole other book, but simplified it incorporates such circumstances as your sex, country of birth, economic status and of course those who you agree to live out this incarnation in agreement with such as your parents, sibling and so forth.

Sometimes these agreements call for the child to remember the essence of their soul and in other instances this remembrance is not needed. Remembering will see a child with psychic sensitivities at time WOWing those around them with their precognitive abilities to predict, reiterate past life experiences or to recognise and communicate with the afterlife. Where on this scale does your child sit? Below, I have provided a simple check list which will help you to identify if your child does have any psychic sensitivity.

- Dramatic mood swings, particularly in areas with lots of people such as shopping centres, hospitals and large public events.
- An active dream state including nightmares. Dreams are a form of clairvoyance, the psychic ability associated with seeing.
- Regular unexplained nausea.
- Knowledge of people and events beyond their scope of knowledge base. For example, talking about Grandma in detail and even being able to describe her appearance even though they have never met.
- Unexplainable tiredness.

If your child exhibits any or all of these occurrences, it is likely that your son or daughter is highly sensitive to energy. This incorporates being sensitive to the energies of this world as much as the energies of the Spirit world. There are the energy and emotions of those we live with, whether suppressed or not. There are the energies of those we love and care for, living or in Spirit as we always carry with us a part of those we are connected to. There are the energies of the world beyond our homes; school, shopping centres, hospitals and even the energies projected by what we watch on TV, just to name a few. A sensitive child is soaking all this of up and is often overwhelmed by it. If there is one thing I have learnt working as a psychic medium and being a mum to Nathan, who is now seventeen, and Jessica, fourteen, is that most adults struggle to understand their own emotions, yet we often expect our children to understand theirs. This is even more difficult for the psychic child, as the lines between their own emotions and that of others is blurred.

Left unrecognised the psychic child can become withdrawn, lonely and often confused as they struggle daily with their emotions. This becomes even more evident for the teenage sensitive and can often lead to depression. Over the years, guiding my own children, combined with having assisted many parents to understand what is happening for their children. I have come to understand there are some commons signs to look for, such as the ones above which can easily overlooked, as not every psychically sensitive child is talking to dead people or predicting the next baby in the family.

As parents, how can we assist, guide and nurture this aspect of your child? This can be done even if you have no psychic tendencies yourself or may not fully understand yourself what it is to be openly sensitive in this way. First and foremost, it is important to acknowledge and validate for them how they are feeling. Just because we may not be able to relate or understand it, it doesn't make it wrong or not real for them. Your child's perception is their reality, so let's help them understand it. This can be achieved quite easily by just taking the time to talk with them about how they are feeling. Get them talking and communicating about their emotions with an aim to just listen and empathise. Often it is enough just for you to listen.

Secondly, there are some simple techniques you can use to assist them in raising their awareness about energies and gaining some management and control of them. This is where a journal or a scrapbook can be an effective tool. Have your son or daughter write or even draw their feelings, dreams and experiences in the journal. Just having an avenue to express it all is extremely beneficial. Then, once you are both comfortable with this and are ready to understand where the emotions come from, whether they be your child's emotions or that of another who may be living or passed. As they write about how they feel, move gently into asking the question why they feel that way, including the question *"Is this emotion mine or someone else's?"* If it is someone else's then ask, *"Whose emotion is this?"* Trust in the answers which come, as for a sensitive child their intuition is strong and highly attuned.

Please remember that what they feel and express and the reasons behind it, are their reality. There is no right or wrong here, so our task is predominantly to listen and guide where we can.

Should your child be experiencing Spirit visitations and psychic occurrences that are causing them to be unsettled and fearful at times, then you might find some of these suggestions helpful:

- Have your child artistically create a door sign for their bedroom titled *"No Spirits allowed!"* Similar to the sign that says *"No boys/girls allowed"*, this will empower them to assert their own energies gaining some control and will let the Spirit world clearly know how they feel. Plus, it will lighten the situation and even make it a little fun for your young medium.
- Every now and then when they are restless and unsettled, cleanse their bedroom by smudging it with the herb sage as described in an earlier chapter. It won't hurt to cleanse the whole house at the same time, all with the added intention of cleansing the energies of all negativity, allowing more love to flow through the energies of your home.
- Cleansing their aura will also help immensely.
- My children prefer to move their bedroom furniture around which also helps in releasing the stale, old negative energy. And they usually intuitively know when this needs to be done.
- Lastly, children will often feel safer praying to their guardian angel or even a loved family member who is in Spirit. So encourage this in their bedtime ritual.

Long term, if children understand that their energy is intricately entwined with the energy of others right from the earliest stages of their existence, this will have the human race evolve with a more spiritually conscious focus, allowing us to live in the knowing that we are all connected and that if we hurt another living being, be it human, animal or plant we recognise that we hurt ourselves. In comparison, if we love another, lift up another and nurture another then in so doing, we are loving and nurturing ourselves as well.

In this chapter:
- Psychic children easily recognize, more than adults that we exist in the world of energy first and are born into this world as a likeness and the human expression of who we are as a soul.
- Psychic children are affected by our multi-faceted environments. It is difficult for a psychic child to understand their own emotions and to separate from what is and isn't theirs.
- Your child's perception is their reality.
- Journaling is a useful tool for a psychic child.

Servitude is more than an Attitude

> We can do no great things, only small things with great love.
> ~**Mother Teresa.**

Before I began writing this book my original intention was to teach what I know about mediumship hoping, you may gain some new techniques and insight to assist with unfolding your psychic abilities and communicating with Spirit. How this book has evolved through allowing the flow of Spirit has seen this intention met, yet it is in my view surpassing that expectation. Whether you go ahead and actually develop competent mediumship abilities or not, this book and the interwoven personal journey I have felt a need to share, now has the ability to inspire on many levels much more than only the mediumship aspects.

Over the years and especially since establishing the Australian College of Mediumship, I have found that there were many challenges and personal learnings I needed to experience to find peace and become the best me I can be. This is the true message of this book. Overcoming your adversity to find within yourself the strength, passion and guiding light we can all be.

When we ignite our spirituality and choose to work with our spiritual abilities, we often do so out of a sense of wanting to help others. This is true in part, however the greater sense within our own soul is that we, ourselves, need the greatest help. As humans with a natural fear of self, we just happen to find it easier to achieve if its disguised as helping another soul.

This is true for myself and for the many, many people who have crossed my path wanting to share their spiritual abilities with others. Even the journey of writing this book, wanting to share information and knowledge with others has unfolded a culmination of being able to see myself as the light of love Gods knows me to be. Once we reach this understanding, only then can our work as a medium truly become about being that light for others.

In the early days of establishing ACOM there was lots of excitement, inspiration, wonder and hope as I and its members flowed along enjoying the community we were creating. It was beautiful to watch people grow and blossom, and I was always fascinated to receive each new piece of inspiration from Spirit. I still am really! Its one of the greatest gifts there is, to receive an inspiration and then see it come into being. I just love that. I digress, however.

Overtime, the experience of ACOM and more importantly the personal journey of learning I was going through began to take its toll. Firstly, there was a lot of betrayal and judgement from others as I learnt I was naïve, too trusting and just wanted to be everyones best friend. Not very workable attributes to have operating a business and especially one that comes with a public profile. Each act of betrayal tore at my heart and battered my self-worth until the last straw, which came in the form of a student who ingratiated herself, offering support and taking on the beginnings of being a teacher. Within a matter of weeks after receiving this opportunity she came to me saying she would be leaving at the end of term as it was just time for her to move on. It wasn't long before some other students from her class began leaving as well. My intuition knew something wasn't right, however sometimes your hands are tied as to what to do. It wasn't until she began denigrating my name in the class that I asked her to finish up immediately. Eventually, the truth came out that she and the others had left to set up their own spiritual development center.

Now please don't miss understand, I have no problem with people genuinely growing and becoming experts in their own right and will even support their efforts to forge a career of their own. This was not what was happening here. Literally, these people had minimal experience and would begin by trying to take my clients, continue to denigrate my name but yet were happy to take my teachings and most of how ACOM operated to set up their own establishment.

This was not the only hurtful experience I encountered during these times, but it was the straw which broke the camels back. What compounded some of the hurt was my sense of belief to forgive others and my belief in personal responsibility. To look within and see how I contributed. How did I attract this? What was it I needed to learn? Was I meant to continue doing this work? On top of this, my sense of responsibility towards the public was also hard to deal with. How easy is it for a five minute expert to set themselves up as an expert using my intellectual property and yet knowing there wasn't a lot I could do about it, if I wanted to maintain my own integrity.

It was after this, that looking back I believe my own soul must of said 'enough is enough'. Time to retreat a little, heal and recover what was lost. Which largely, was my self worth and belief in myself as a medium. In time, I couldn't financially sustain the center, letting go of the premises and the larger ACOM community at the end of 2008.

This act in itself was for me another painful experience, having to face one of my biggest fears. Having found my purpose and what I believe is my life's work, to let go of what I had worked so hard at creating was extremely difficult even though I knew I had the support of Spirit, my family and my close friends. I came to see that it wasn't really an ending as opposed to making room for what was next, allowing my work to change and evolve in new ways which were more in alignment with who I had become.

Since then and just by putting one foot in front of the other, I have healed and am much richer for all of it. I can honestly say that my self worth is stronger and far more unshakeable than it was prior to all of this. Even just the other day I was speaking with a publisher regarding their option to decline publishing this book. I said to them that *"I respectfully disagree with their view that the writing isn't strong enough"* and walked away thinking *"their loss"*. Don't get me wrong, its not that I think this book is better than anyone elses, I share this because it reflects the strength of my self belief now. Not too long ago I would have taken it on, become melancholy and spiralled my thinking into *"OMG, I'm not good enough."* So now it's *"I am woman, hear me roar!"*

In serving your own Spirit first above all else, you will find a deep seated connection naturally evolves to that part of you connected to the Divine and you develop an understanding of all that goes with that. Only then with this foundation can one truly serve the Spirit of another through mediumship, be it the Spirit of the living or those in the Spirit world.

I share with you one final life experience which hit home the true understanding of servitude that I needed and released me from my self limiting beliefs about my worthiness as a medium. Last year in the middle of writing this book I travelled to the United States to attend two consecutive workshops on mediumship facilitated by three internationally acclaimed mediums. The initial weekend with all three in attendance was inspiring to say the least. It was fun with a great mix of styles from the presenters as they shared their knowledge, experience and abilities. I made a new life long friendship and even received a reading from Mavis, one of the teachers who is a UK medium with over thirty years of experience and regularly teaches at the Arthur Finlay College. The weekend workshop provided a great deal of inspiration as I admired the humbleness and deep sense of servitude exhibited by these UK mediums.

I was scheduled to stay on through the week to attend an additional five day workshop, though I would soon find my time at this workshop cut short. In contrast to the weekend, I found the presenter of this workshop rude, condescending and approaching the whole experience with a lack of humbleness and a distinct lack of the servitude compared to that we had all witnessed over the weekend. There were many specific examples of this behaviour I could share, however what is important for me to share is what I gained from the experience and how I responded.

Early in the week, myself and my new friend decided to leave the workshop and not return. Taking myself out of this situation and asking for a refund was the best I could do to show that what was happening was unacceptable in my view and to minimise the negativity I could feel building. I did not want to sit in the workshop all week and have this fester. I often take on too much responsibility caring for everyone else first, especially when I believe something to be wrong and when it comes to how Spirit is being represented. This time however, I needed to take care of myself first. Throughout this week, I started to see how I always feel the need 'to do the right thing' allowing other people's expectations to influence my choices. And yet again, I also learnt, how easy it is for people who you think are a friend to show themselves to be otherwise.

In leaving and asking for a refund, I was taking a stand and showing the universe the kind of medium I am. I was affirming what is acceptable and what isn't and how important it is to walk our talk. In doing so, I came to realise that while I may not or ever have a profile as well known as this guys, what I am bringing to the spiritual community is worthy and deserving of representing Spirit as much as the next medium. In my own way, the message of Spirit will reach those who need it without confusion of displacing the connection of the Divine with expectation and that of maintaining a 'famous' profile.

This whole experience was quite painful to live through due to the shock at being let down in this way, even though I know I wasn't the only one to come away from this workshop with a negative experience. Yet in looking within over the following weeks, it all brought about a monumental shift as I came to understand the level of servitude truly required to serve Spirit and where that really comes from. As I said earlier, this comes from serving your own Spirit first which in turn creates a natural sense to remain humble, focused on healing and living a life in service to Spirit.

Once you have this, your integrity will take care of itself and so too will your humbleness. The energy of Spirit is the essence of all of this, so it stands to reason that if your Mediumship connection is rooted in this foundation, then you will naturally be humble with a high level of truth and integrity where you will be able to live this with relative ease as love becomes all there is and you find yourself living a new kind of normal.

In this chapter:
- Developing and exploring your mediumship is a journey of self discovery that involves self awareness, self responsibility and healing, overcoming adversity and finding within yourself the strength, passion and the guiding light to be the best you that you can be!

Acknowledgements

Writing a book such as this not only takes the two years from when I put pen to paper to having it available for you to read, it also takes many more years of life experience full of some very special people who deserve my thankyou and the recognition of having a hand in *A New Kind of Normal* coming together.

The first thankyou must go to my family, Rod, Nathan and Jessica. I am blessed to have you all by my side as we walk this journey that at times can be challenging as much as it is unique. From the bottom of my heart, I am grateful for your love, support and patience. I love you all and thank you.

Mum, your heart is healing in small immeasurable ways which is just right for you and I am blessed to be able to share in all that with you. Thank you for being you and may I never stop needing my mum. I love you.

To my brother Allen, we miss you and love you, knowing you forever hold a place in our hearts and now in this book too. Keep up the good work!

John Lynch, without you my thoughts and beliefs on the afterlife may have never evolved to where they are, beyond the norm and in a lot of ways helping to break down barriers just like you did from your place in the afterlife. Thank you.

The journey so far has at times been a big challenge often made easier by some very loving and supportive friends. Nicole Psaroudis, Sophie Cram, Rita Maher, Nicolle Poll, Monique Allerton, Mark Webster and Shawn De bord. I am blessed to know you and call you friend. Thank you.

An extra special thank you must go to Nicolle Poll for all of your editing and guidance in putting this book together. I couldn't have done it without you. Thank you.

To Peggy McColl, meeting you was a significant turning point in my spiritual development and self belief. I am forever grateful for the work you do and rejoice in knowing you. Thank you.

To Trish Mclaughlin, I am so grateful that you were my first spiritual development teacher and am honoured to still call you a mentor. You have always been one of the rare people who can challenge my thinking, which I love and I have the utmost respect for your integrity, your mediumship and your sense of self. You'll be pleased to know I finally stopped being so hard on myself.

This book was rebirthed and evolved into its final form after spending a special day towards the end of 2010 with Lucy Cavendish. I am forever grateful for the awareness and inspiration you and your workshop provided to finally bring it all to life. I showed up!

To each and every person who stepped through the doors of ACOM, thank you for sharing part of your journey with me. Our coming together taught me so much about myself, my mediumship and my connection to the Divine and for that I am wholeheartedly grateful. Thank you.

To you the reader, I thank you for sharing in my work. I know I connect and meet wonderfully passionate people through my work so I am sure this is you too. For you, I wish a life filled with love, joy and Spirit.

Lastly, I thank God and all those in Spirit who have guided and supported me. My connection to you is the source of all that I am and will be. Thankyou.

About the Author

Kerrie Wearing is an author, soul coach and medium who lives in Sydney, Australia with her husband, two teenage children and two dogs. Kerrie is passionate about helping people finding the spirit within and coaching them to live the life we all deserve to live.

She is founder and managing director of inSpirit Publishing, managing editor of inSpirit Magazine, the creator and co-host of Paracon Australia, a member and volunteer events co-ordinator for CIEMA Inc while also conducting a successful mediumship coaching business.

Kerrie invites your contact via her website:
www.psychicmedium.com.au

www.ingramcontent.com/pod-product-compliance
Lightning Source LLC
Chambersburg PA
CBHW071205160426
43196CB00011B/2202